GW00419694

A HANDBOOK OF FAITHS
the beliefs and practices of people
of different faiths and cultures

Cover Design by: Creative Touch Design
Printed by: Genesis Europrint, U.K.

ISBN 1 902360 10 9

PREFACE

We live in a world of difference - different cultures, different histories, different faiths. For many people, these differences are cause for celebration and learning. Recognising an alternative perspective on the world can open our eyes to fresh ways of seeing things. It can enrich our experience of the world. We do this, not by merging everything together and losing difference, but – precisely the opposite – by taking time to respect each other's standpoints; to try and understand what these traditions are; from where they came; what codes of conduct they apply; to recognise that each of our own traditions and beliefs – which we take for granted – are strange in the eyes of someone from another background.

Yet we also live in a world in which fear and suspicion of alternative viewpoints is sadly too prevalent. As this edition is published we are all too aware of the global and cultural tensions that exist and the significant dangers which these create. We can be filled with data across the world in an instant. Yet how many of us can really say we understand each other's point of view?

I am delighted to welcome this edition of the SIFRE Handbook. The first step in understanding is to be able to have respect for each other's faiths. And that respect can only be demonstrated in practical ways – by knowing about diet or forms of address or how certain critical events in life are handled in different traditions. Most of us want to show respect for each other but can easily fail to do so through ignorance or oversight. SIFRE performs an invaluable service in Suffolk and beyond in building understanding. The handbook provides in a unique and accessible way key information which assists any of us – in communities, in public service, in commercial and social activity – in building and maintaining respectful and good relationships. Thank you to SIFRE for this important Handbook.

Mike More
Chief Executive of Suffolk County Council
November 2005

FOREWORD

Suffolk Inter-Faith Resource published the first edition of this handbook in 1998, incorporating guidelines that East Suffolk Local Health Services NHS Trust had produced for its Staff and Carers. The second edition was published in 2001 after consultation with the Ipswich Hospital, Suffolk Social Care Services and with other professional and voluntary groups working in the community. A third edition followed in 2003.

We are now publishing the fourth edition with revised and expanded contents. We continue to have in mind the requirements of people working in the public services and in the private and voluntary sectors. We also commend the book to all those who are interested in knowing more about the faiths and traditions of those who live around them.

We are aware that there is now a proliferation of guidelines, handbooks, "toolkits" and web-sites dealing with cultural and religious diversity. We have been asked to contribute to, or comment on, some of them and we have scrutinised others which we have come across. Some of them are very good but some are rather weak and contain misleading information. We think it is important for people to write about themselves and so this publication is a collaborative effort. Members of the faiths prepared or revised their own sections but each contribution was submitted to others for their comments and advice.

Difficult decisions had to be made regarding what to include and what to omit. No handbook would ever be long enough but it was important to be concise. Fuller information about the beliefs and practices of faith communities is available from us at the SIFRE Centre, within Suffolk College and members of SIFRE are happy to be consulted about issues concerning their faiths and cultures. We are happy also to be publishing this in association with The Festival Shop who have, for many years, provided resources around multifaith, multicultural and citizenship issues.

The Handbook of Faiths represents close co-operation over many years between people of different faiths who have come to know and respect each other, who work together in the community and who are engaged in a mutual learning process.

Cynthia M Capey,
Hon Faiths Officer,
Suffolk Inter-Faith Resource.
November 2005

CONTENTS

INTRODUCTION

The communities in which we live today are composed of so many diverse groups that conventions which used to guide our lives can no longer be relied upon as a framework. We find it hard to distinguish between religious and cultural differences and so can very easily jump to the wrong conclusions. We may not even know the answers to some basic questions.

What should we call people? Can we use their first name or would they prefer a more formal style like Mr and Mrs or Ms? How should we address a Sikh or a Muslim? If we are visiting new neighbours or clients should we take off our shoes? Do we need to cover our arms or legs? Does modesty matter? Is it polite to look someone in the eye? This handbook does not attempt to answer all such questions, but it highlights some important aspects, alongside some background information and basic principles.

For a start, it is helpful to remember that while our dating system may be based on Christianity, other faiths and cultures have their own calendars, new years and festivals which give significance to their lives and require families to get together, adults to miss work or children to be away from school. In recognition of this diversity many people prefer to use CE and BCE (Common Era, and Before the Common Era) rather than BC and AD.

People may have set times for prayer. They may have special rituals to mark the various stages of life. Particular attention must be paid to dietary requirements. All aspects of food preparation need to be respected. Special arrangements may need to be made to accommodate individual needs.

When people of different religious and cultural backgrounds meet each other they may gain new perspectives on life or recall forgotten values. Most faiths acknowledge that every part of life is sacred and that reverence should be shown to all people and to the whole natural world. Putting one's hands together and bowing one's head, as Hindus, Sikhs and others do in greeting, is to honour the divine in the other person. Removing one's shoes when entering a house may be a sign that the home also is seen as a holy place.

Such considerations may pave the way for meeting people from different cultural and religious backgrounds but we must beware of stereotyping. Nobody can be neatly categorised! Certainly we can tell very little about each other from the colour of our skins. Our religious and cultural backgrounds, our individual experiences and our aspirations may be harder to discern, but they can have far more influence on us.

AFRICAN CARIBBEAN COMMUNITY

There have been people from the Caribbean in Britain since the 17th century, but the majority of migrants came by invitation to Britain during the 1950s and early 1960s. They came in response to a shortage of manual labour, expecting that they would eventually return to their own island. 60% of African Caribbean people in the UK are of Jamaican descent.

Each Caribbean island has its own identity and people do not necessarily feel any affiliation towards the other islands. Religion plays an important role in people's lives, particularly for the older generation. Rastafarianism is a religion specific to this community. There are Muslims and Buddhists. However, the majority are Christian, and belong to various denominations including Seventh-day Adventists and Pentecostals. Some prefer to attend black-led churches. Roman Catholicism predominated in those islands formerly under Spanish or French influences, and Protestantism prevailed elsewhere.

Attending church on Sunday is a big occasion for which people expect to dress smartly. Gospel music is an important part of the culture. The Church is a great source of support in times of illness, poverty or distress.

BIRTH

It is expected that babies will be christened around the age of six weeks and that children will be confirmed by the age of 11. If these customs are not followed, the family may feel ill at ease within the community. Abortion is considered repugnant by many African Caribbean women. In cases of divorce there is often a strong feeling of shame, and also concern about being rebuked by members of the family and the church.

DEATH

People prefer to die at home with their family around them. Funerals tend to be big affairs. Families are usually prepared to contribute to the cost. Coffins are open for family and friends to view in the church.

DIET

The typical Caribbean diet includes yams, rice, okra, breadfruit, cassava and maize, plantains and bananas. Spices are widely used. Fish, chicken and goat meat are popular meats. Pork is not acceptable for Rastafarians and Seventh-day Adventists.

FAMILY VALUES

Traditionally women have had a leading role in the home. This is reflected in the fact that sometimes the family name passes along the mother's line. Members of the older generation are held in respect by the younger and often prefer to be addressed as Mr and Mrs.

Grandmothers have traditionally had a significant role within the family, often bearing the main responsibility for the upbringing of the grandchildren, enabling the mother to work. Older people support each other, share produce and help out in times of trouble – doing jobs and delivering meals to people's homes. Those living alone will often be invited out to meals.

HYGIENE AND HEALTH

Personal privacy should be respected. Cleanliness is very important and great attention is paid to care of the skin and hair. Pick style combs are used and cocoa butter or coal tar shampoo preferred. Vaseline mixed with olive oil or castor oil may be used for the hair and skin. Some people will treat their whole body with unguents every day, and their hair at least once a week.

Generally black people find it hard to discuss physical ailments with strangers and there is a tradition of keeping personal issues in the family. Most people are prepared to consult GPs, but illness is often viewed as a punishment.

Sickle cell anaemia is an inherited disease specific to this community and the incidence of hypertension, strokes and diabetes has been found to be higher among the African Caribbean population than among the population in general.

Footnote:

The above notes apply more to the older members of the African Caribbean community than to the younger generation.

For more information on the faiths of African Caribbean people see other sections of this handbook.

ASYLUM SEEKERS
AND REFUGEES

Asylum seekers and refugees are unlike the other groups listed in this handbook in that they are not a group defined by one particular faith or cultural background, but rather by their status as victims of oppression. Therefore they come from a diverse range of faiths, cultures and backgrounds.

The movement of asylum seekers is like a mirror reflecting the world's hot-spots, an indicator of war, conflict and oppression. In July 2004 the majority of asylum seekers entering the UK were Muslims from the Middle East especially from Iraq and Iran. Previously there were many fleeing Afghanistan. Since then there are increasing numbers from East and North Africa from countries such as Sudan and Liberia.

According to the 1951 UN Convention on the status of refugees, a refugee is defined as "A person who, owing to a well-founded fear of being persecuted for reason of race, religion, nationality, membership of a particular social group or political opinion, is outside the country of nationality and is unable or, owing to such fear, unwilling to return to it."

People who are requesting refugee status are normally called asylum seekers. Once they have been granted leave to stay, their immediate family members may join them. However, the urgent circumstances in which many refugees have to leave their homes mean that families are often split up. For example, if there is only enough money for one person to travel, it will often be the man of the household who goes on ahead, in order to try to find a safe haven where he can earn enough money to have his family join him. This is especially true of Islamic and other traditional societies, who would often be reluctant to send a woman on her own to a country where she does not know the language, is unprotected, and does not have her usual support network of friends, neighbours and extended family. This explains why the majority of asylum seekers in the UK are young men who have travelled on their own.

There are many other problems for refugee communities. These include language difficulties, culture shock, different climate, difficulties with accommodation, unfamiliar diet, unsuitable clothing, lack of money, feelings of isolation from starting life again in an unfamiliar and very different place and the fact that they face much negativity from both the press and the public in general. Many of the refugees have faced persecution in one form or another, as well as varying degrees of physical and psychological trauma and, in some cases, torture. Many refugees feel insecure because of the separation from their families and uncertain legal status. Consequently, mental health is one of the most important health problems that affect refugees. If asylum seekers are not allowed to work and are leading isolated lives in this country their mental health may suffer even more.

All public service providers should be aware that refugees may be wary of people in authority, and may react badly to uniforms. They may feel that by discussing problems and being open about the past they will jeopardise their situation. Refugees need support and advice in accessing public services in an unfamiliar country. Language problems can compound potential difficulties in becoming familiar with procedures in the UK.

There are various support systems in every region of the UK. For example, the Eastern Region has a Refugee Council One Stop Service based in Ipswich that can advise on issues that concern refugees and asylum seekers. It can also help service providers to access translating services and other helpful bodies. The Refugee Council is funded by central government, and so works within a strict remit and is not allowed to provide help for destitute asylum seekers. However, there are other charitable bodies that may be able to provide support. For example, the Suffolk Refugee Support Forum, based in Ipswich, provides complementary services to the Refugee Council. Other regions have similar organisations.

BAHÁ'ÍS

The Bahá'í Faith was founded in the 19th century by Bahá'u'lláh, who was born in Persia (modern day Iran) and is honoured by Bahá'ís as the latest in a line of messengers from God that includes Zoroaster, Krishna, Abraham, Moses, the Buddha, Jesus and Muhammad. This continuity is reflected in Bahá'u'lláh's teachings, which stress the oneness of the world's religions, and the oneness of humankind. Bahá'ís strive to abolish all prejudices and to gain equality for all, regardless of race or sex. Bahá'ís have no priesthood or liturgy. They come from many different cultural, racial, social and religious backgrounds and support democratically elected institutions at local, national and international levels. They are required to obey the government but may choose to abstain from partisan politics, which can be seen as creating disunity in the community. Bahá'ís integrate scientific attitudes into their faith and have an holistic approach to life.

ABLUTIONS AND OBLIGATORY PRAYER

Bahá'ís should perform ritual washing before reciting the obligatory prayer. If water is not available or cannot be applied to the hands and the face, the believer may recite 5 times the verse "In the name of God, the Most Pure, the Most Pure". The obligatory prayer is performed facing the holy shrine at Bahji in Israel. There are alternative forms of obligatory prayer. In the West the short form is usually recited, once in 24 hours, between noon and sunset. Those who are ill or over 70 are exempt. Menstruating women are exempt if they recite 95 times "Glorified be God, the Lord of Splendour and Beauty".

BIRTH

Bahá'ís believe that the soul comes into being at conception. Methods of contraception that prevent implantation of the fertilised ovum are considered unacceptable. Sterilisation and abortion are forbidden except on compelling medical grounds.

DEATH

The dead body should be washed and wrapped in a shroud of cotton or silk. A special ring is placed on the finger and the corpse is laid in a wooden coffin. Bahá'ís may not be cremated or embalmed and may not be buried more than an hour's journey from the place of death.

DIET

Bahá'ís do not normally drink alcohol, but may take it within medicine prescribed by doctors. They practise moderation in diet. Some Bahá'ís are vegetarian.

FASTING

During the fasting period (March 2-20), Bahá'ís may not eat or drink between sunrise and sunset. Fasting is not obligatory for those under 15 or over 70, for menstruating, pregnant or nursing women, for the sick or for travellers.

FESTIVALS

The Bahá'í New Year (Naw-Ruz) is on 21st March. No work is done on this day, and Bahá'ís may wish to be at home for this occasion. The period leading up to Naw-Ruz (2-20 March) is a period of reflection and preparation for the coming year, and it is marked by fasting. Another important festival period is Ridvan, from 21st April to 2nd May. This celebrates Baha'u'llah's declaration of his mission. The 1st, 9th and 12th days within this festival are holy days on which work is suspended.

GREETING

Some Bahá'ís might shake hands, some might bow, some might hug close friends. Often Bahá'ís will greet each other by saying "Alláh-u-Abhá".

IN BAHÁ'Í HOMES

There may be a plaque with the Arabic inscription "Ya Bahá'u'l-Abhá" ("O Glory of the All Glorious").

MARRIAGE

There is no set form of marriage but the following obligatory sentence must be said in front of witnesses: "We will all verily abide by the will of God." Bahá'ís have free choice in marriage, but parental consent is sought to help create unity between the two families.

MEDICAL PROCEDURES

Blood transfusions and organ donations are allowed.

BUDDHISTS

The various Buddhist traditions have their origin in what was then northern India and stem from the enlightenment of Siddhartha Gautama who is said to have been born in 563BCE. Although he was a prince, he left his comfortable home in search of the Truth to bring to an end the misery which he could see all around him. He experienced a profound spiritual realisation: the ability to see things as they really are, the inter-dependence of all things and the inevitable link between the conditions we create and their consequences. Thus he became a Buddha (one who has awakened as though from a dream). He spent the next 45 years travelling through northern India communicating this liberating vision.

Buddhism has been described as a "non-theistic religion" because there is no place for an all-powerful creator God within it. Some Buddhists revere the Buddha as though he was divine, but Gautama himself was a human being who gained enlightenment through his own efforts. All Buddhists believe that there have been many Buddhas in the past, present and future and that all living beings have the potential to become Buddhas. They can do this by aiming to reach enlightenment, by following the Buddhist way of life. Buddhists value compassion, selflessness, personal responsibility, and mindfulness of the present moment. They try to avoid causing harm to any life form.

The 'Three Jewels' of Buddhism are the Buddha, the dharma (his teachings) and the sangha, or community of Buddhists. It is essential for Buddhists to retain close contact with the sangha at all times. Although Buddhists come from a broad range of cultural backgrounds, in the UK most Buddhists are western converts.

BIRTH

Buddhist ethics proceed on a "case by case" basis, but there are general principles. For example, contraception can include pills to prevent conception but not morning-after pills. If sexual intercourse has taken place, then full responsibility must be taken for the possible consequences, including parenthood. The first precept of Buddhism (abstain from taking life) makes abortion unacceptable unless the mother's life is at stake. There are no set rituals for the birth of a child but the occasion could be marked by a family celebration. Parents might take the baby to a temple to be blessed by monks.

CLOTHING

Buddhists are likely to dress modestly. Buddhist monks or nuns often wear orange robes and have shaved heads. One of the monastic rules is not to become separated from one's robes.

DEATH

Acceptance of death is a key part of Buddhist philosophy. Buddhism teaches that the ideal death is a calm, fully conscious one. A Buddhist will require support from his or her spiritual master. In terminal cases Buddhists may refuse painkillers. They may need support in deciding what level of medication would be appropriate. An atmosphere of calm should be promoted around a dying Buddhist – the presence of distressed relatives may not be conducive to the desired tranquillity.

When a Buddhist dies it is important that a Buddhist minister is informed. Ideally the body should be moved as little as possible before he arrives. Between three and seven days should elapse before the body is disposed of, as some Buddhists believe that consciousness remains in the body for a while after death. This belief in continued consciousness means that Buddhists treat the newly dead as if they were still alive, and would prefer medical staff to do so also, explaining their procedures as they handle the body. Ceremonies for the dead include chanting and meditation.

Both cremation and burial are acceptable as, traditionally, bodies could be disposed of by means of any of the four elements, earth, air, fire or water. As some Buddhists believe that spiritual death may take place some time after organic death, it may not be possible for the organs of a deceased Buddhist to be donated. However, many Buddhists would feel that the compassionate act of donating organs outweighs concerns about disturbing the body.

Some Buddhists believe in literal reincarnation, whereas others believe in a spiritual rebirth that is understood as a causal connection between lives, rather than the reincarnation of an unchanging individual soul. Some would say that the habitual patterns of the mind continue through different births. This is often imaged as a line of candles, each lit from the previous one.

DIET

There are no absolute rules for lay Buddhists concerning diet. Many Buddhists are vegetarian or vegan, in accordance with the first Buddhist precept – abstain from taking life. A monk should eat anything that is offered to him, because of the benefit in encouraging the generosity of the giver, but would be gravely at fault for hinting that he would like meat. Monks and nuns, or other Buddhists who are especially concerned with shrines or images should avoid onions and garlic because of the smell.

FASTING

In the West, it is mostly only monks and nuns who fast. On fast days a Buddhist may eat before noon, but not afterwards. Full moon days and new moon days are often fast days for Buddhists.

FESTIVALS

A commonly observed festival is Wesak, or Bodhi Day, the Buddha's birthday.

GREETING

In Buddhist countries the normal form of greeting is to place the hands together in a prayerful manner and bow. Buddhists in Western countries normally adopt the usual styles of greeting found there, like shaking hands. When greeting a monk or a nun, it is not appropriate to take their hand or embrace them.

IN A BUDDHIST HOME

Most Buddhist homes will have a shrine, probably with a statue of the Buddha. Some Buddhists might prefer visitors to remove their shoes when entering the home. Many Buddhists would prefer that Dharma books are not laid directly on the floor, or stepped over, or have other objects placed on top of them.

HEALTH AND HYGIENE

Many Buddhists prefer showers to baths. A Buddhist may wish to sleep on the floor.

Traditionally Buddhists treat doctors with respect. However, since much emphasis is put on the importance of having a clear mind, Buddhists may be reluctant to take medications that are mind-altering, and will need side-effects explained to them thoroughly.

Buddhists may prefer the use of home remedies - for example, rice porridge (one part rice to two parts water) may be considered beneficial for convalescence.

Buddhist monks and nuns would prefer to be treated by members of the same sex.

PUJA

The terms 'prayer' and 'worship' are not really appropriate to Buddhism, since there is no God figure. 'Puja', meaning 'the acknowledgement of an ideal' is better, though not all Buddhists will use or be familiar with this term. Some Buddhists use the word 'prayer' to mean a devout personal determination, without the connotation of praying to a deity. A space should be set aside for puja, which may involve chanting. Incense, flowers and candles may be used. Buddhists wash before puja. A Buddhist temple is called a vihara. When entering a Buddhist centre, visitors will be expected to remove their shoes. Some Buddhists consider pointing the sole of the foot at the figure of Buddha disrespectful.

CHINESE

M ost Chinese people living in Britain originate from Hong Kong, but there are others from mainland China, Malaysia, Singapore, Mauritius, Vietnam and Fiji. The majority are from a Buddhist tradition but do not adhere strictly to traditional Buddhist practices, for various reasons, both historical and cultural. A significant minority follow Taoism, the traditional popular religion of China. Some may come from Christian backgrounds, both Protestant and Catholic. There are also Chinese Muslims. In general, Chinese people are likely to draw on Buddhist, Taoist and Confucianist traditions.

There are different cultural backgrounds and languages within the Chinese community. All the different groups are likely to practise customs associated with reverence for ancestors. As with many migrant communities, the second generation may not follow their parents' beliefs. The official language of China is Mandarin but Cantonese is more commonly spoken. However, although a Cantonese speaker listening to a Mandarin speaker might not understand anything said, they could probably read what was written.

BIRTH

It is traditional for a Chinese woman to stay at home for a month after childbirth. She may not even want to go for a bath during the first few days after giving birth as this also would disturb the traditional resting time. It is also the case that immersion is sometimes regarded as bad for the health.

Fathers are rarely present at births. Relatives mark a birth by giving money in red envelopes. Boys are often preferred to girls.

DEATH

Death and bereavement are very much shared experiences and both the dying and the bereaved receive much comfort and support. To die alone, or without issue, is considered a very sad fate for a Chinese person. Relatives and friends may wish to see the body before the coffin is closed. They may arrange for the body or ashes to be sent back to their place of origin, sometimes to be incorporated into an ancestor's grave. Death is an important time for ceremony, and the rituals, which vary considerably among the Chinese community, may last for up to a week. White is the colour of mourning. Crying aloud to demonstrate grief is common.

DIET

Diet is influenced to a certain extent by the cultural belief that good health is related to the balance of the physical elements of the body. Therefore Chinese people are likely to want food with opposing qualities: something sweet with something sour; something hot with something cold; and so on. Rice is the staple diet with lots of freshly cooked vegetables, fish and very little meat. Most Chinese people do not eat beef or lamb. Some, especially Buddhists, are vegetarian and some follow a vegetarian diet on certain days of the month. Milk is not usually included in the diet.

Freshly prepared food is preferred at all times and Chinese people tend to have a strong preference for home cooking. Like other minority groups, they may ask relatives to bring food into hospital for them as they have definite customs relating to the preparation of food and to the manner in which it is eaten. Ginger is an important ingredient especially when people are ill.

FAMILY LIFE

A person's family is of great significance. It is important to have a son to become head of the family and to carry on the family name. It may not be acceptable for people originating from the same village or clan to marry. Families work together and pool their money. Great respect is shown to the elders and it is traditional for the children to look after their parents in old age. Chinese households are often extended families. However, some older people do not speak English and can become socially isolated.

Chinese society expects little emotional display or physical contact, even between parents and children. Expressions of loyalty and affection are more likely to be practical, for example gifts, especially money in red envelopes.

Efforts are sometimes made to suppress left-handedness in children. This is a matter of social conformity, rather than a specific taboo. For example, Chinese people traditionally use the right hand to hold chopsticks, so left-handed people might clash with their neighbours at the table.

FESTIVALS

The most significant festival is the Chinese New Year (Yuan Tan). It is celebrated in Jan/Feb. Business accounts should be settled and all debts paid before the New Year. It is everyone's birthday and everyone becomes a year older. On New Year's Eve everyone is supposed to return to the family home for a reunion dinner. On the first day of the New Year, young people go to pay respects to the older generation, and prayers are offered to the dead. The festivities come to a close on the 15th day with Yuan Sin, the Lantern Festival. In the UK, celebrations last from one new moon to the next.

Other important festivals are Ching Ming, the Festival of Pure Brightness (April), Dragon Boat Festival (June), and the mid-Autumn Festival of Moon Cake (September). At Chung Yuan, the Festival of Hungry Ghosts (October), paper objects are made to aid the dead who have no resting places or descendants, and paper boats are burnt at temples to help the dead on their way.

GREETINGS

When greeting each other, many Chinese people will place their hands together in a prayerful attitude and bow. When greeting a western person they would use western customs.

HEALTH AND HYGIENE

Chinese people usually prefer showering or a sponge-down to bathing.

Any illness or disability is considered bad luck but medical treatment or an operation to correct this will be acceptable. Visitors to hospital may be given a red packet containing money so that they will not take the bad luck to their homes. There is frequently a great apprehension amongst the older generation about operations of any kind, and a widespread dislike of giving blood samples. The tradition of Chinese medicine is very ancient. Preference for western or traditional medicine may vary with age and upbringing. Medical professionals may need to explain (through an interpreter if necessary) the need for medication, to children and grandchildren as well as to the patient. For example, some elderly people think that the more medicine they take, the quicker they will get better!

HOME

On entering the house, it is often the custom to remove shoes. If you are offered refreshments, it is polite to accept. Some Chinese people may go to great lengths to achieve good feng shui, so care should be taken not to disarrange articles in the home. There may be small statues on display.

MARRIAGE

Match making is practised by some Chinese families. Additionally, the art of astrology may be used to determine when would be the most lucky date for the wedding. Brides traditionally wear red.

MODESTY

As is the case for most women, Chinese women are generally happier being treated or cared for by female professionals. Men usually prefer to be cared for or treated by men.

NAMES AND TITLES

Traditionally the family name is written before the personal name. This may be not be the case for Westernised Chinese people. A person's family of origin is of great significance, so Chinese women often retain their maiden names. Some add their husband's name to their own family name. Children take the father's surname. Through respect for elders, a person would be unlikely to call their parents' friends by their names, but would call them 'aunt' or 'uncle'. A friend of an elder sibling would be addressed as 'older brother' or 'older sister'.

Footnote:

The above notes apply more to the older members of the Chinese community than to the younger generation. For more information on the faiths, see other sections of this handbook.

CHRISTIANS

The Christian faith is founded on the life and teaching of Jesus who lived 2000 years ago in what is modern day Israel/Palestine. Christians believe in One God and worship him as Creator. They believe that God is uniquely revealed in the life, death and resurrection of Jesus and strive to lead an ethical life based on His message of love for all people. The Holy Spirit is revered as the agent of God's activity in the world. The Bible is treasured as a guide, inspiration and source of learning.

In the early days of Christianity there was no formal structure or set pattern of belief or worship. Christianity developed out of Judaism and its first scriptures were Jewish. Christian creeds, liturgies, and patterns of leadership evolved over time. Collections of Christian writings were gradually brought together to form the New Testament.

From about the sixth century C.E. the Western and Eastern Churches began to separate. The split was formalised in the eleventh century. Some of the differences between the churches were theological and some were cultural. Eastern and Western Churches still have different calendars and do not celebrate Christmas and Easter at the same time.

There are increasing numbers of Orthodox Christians in the UK, as a result of various upheavals in Eastern Europe. The Greek Orthodox Church is the largest Orthodox Church in the UK; there are also Russian Orthodox, Antiochian (Arab) Orthodox and Oriental Orthodox churches. They represent many different cultures and languages, and include Greeks, Russians, Serbs, Poles, Ukrainians and Romanians.

The Reformation of the 16th century led to the emergence of Protestant Churches and divided the Western Church into Roman Catholic and Protestant. England became a Protestant country with the Anglican Church as the state religion.

There are now numerous Christian groups within the UK. Some are organised as formal churches and are part of a wider organisation; others are independent house churches which may be linked to a national or international network. It is impossible to cover them all in this handbook. Most are Trinitarian (that is they believe that the One God is known in three persons – God the Father, God the Son and God the Holy Spirit), but a considerable number are not. Unitarians, for example, derive their name from their historic insistence on the Divine Unity.

A number of churches in the UK have made a covenant to work together and support each other. These include Anglicans, Baptists, Methodists, Roman Catholics, Salvation Army, Society of Friends, United Reformed Church and others depending on location. As "Churches Together" they provide chaplaincies in colleges, hospitals and prisons, they join together in social work and community projects, and they sometimes share buildings, especially on new estates. Their common ground is considerable but their practices may diverge, particularly in regard to sacraments like Baptism and Holy Communion, which are not practised by the Salvation Army or the Quakers.

In this section we are focussing on the Western Churches, but we recognise that there are many people in the UK from the Eastern Churches, some of whom are refugees and asylum seekers. There are Coptic Christians, Armenians, Ethiopian Orthodox, Syrian Orthodox and others. There are increasing numbers from Africa. Those individuals who come from churches in other parts of the world may have very different cultural experiences of Christianity and may feel very isolated in this country. Their diversity needs to be acknowledged and their traditions explored.

ANOINTING OF THE SICK

Anointing of the sick is important to Roman Catholics and to those members of the Church of England who are known as Anglo-Catholics. It is imperative to call a priest to anoint the dying, but this sacrament can also be offered to the sick, especially before an operation, as a sign of God's healing power and as a source of comfort. However, for many people, anointing has traditionally been associated with impending death and so the matter needs to be handled sensitively. Children also may wish to be anointed if they are ill. Latter-day Saints anoint the sick with oil alongside prayer.

BAPTISM

Most Christians are baptised, some when they are babies, others when they are adults. In non-conformist churches, where adult baptism by total immersion is the norm, babies may be dedicated or blessed. If the newborn baby of Roman Catholic parents is at risk, the baby should be baptised promptly, ideally by a priest. In an emergency, anyone, even someone who is not a Christian, can perform the baptism, providing they have the right intention and baptise the baby "In the name of the Father, and of the Son, and of the Holy Spirit". Anglicans, Methodists and some other Christian parents with newborn babies at risk may also request baptism – or, in some cases, the naming – of the infant.

BLOOD TRANSFUSIONS

This is of particular importance to Jehovah's Witnesses, for whom blood represents life itself and so must be treated with respect. They carry an Advance Medical Directive/Release that directs no blood transfusions be given under any circumstances, while relieving medical practitioners/hospitals of responsibility for any damages that might be caused by their refusal of blood. When entering the hospital, consent/release forms should be signed stating this and dealing specifically with the hospital care needed.

Non-blood volume expanders are acceptable, and re-infusion of their own blood is permitted by many Witnesses as long as the blood is not stored and providing that the equipment is arranged in a circuit that is constantly linked to the patient's circulatory system. While a blood transfusion is not acceptable, organ donation and transplantation are not forbidden. Therefore, whether to accept an organ transplant is a personal and medical decision and the same would be true of organ donation. So while refusing blood they willingly accept all non-blood alternative medical and surgical management. Also, Witnesses will receive components with no blood – e.g. corneas. The use of minor blood fractions, such as albumin, immunoglobulins and haemophiliac preparations, are a matter of personal choice. If there is doubt, Jehovah's Witnesses' Hospital Liaison Committees can advise.

CIRCUMCISION

Some of the Eastern Churches (eg. Syrian Orthodox) follow the ancient custom of circumcision of boys.

COMMUNION

Communion (Breaking of Bread, Eucharist, Lord's Supper or Mass), like Baptism, goes back to the very early days of the church, to the meals shared by Jesus and his disciples, especially the Last Supper. Communion unites Christians with the death and resurrection of Jesus, and with each other. It can also act as a recommitment to follow in the path set out by Jesus' life and example. Communion services are regularly held in most Christian churches and communion is often taken to sick people in their homes or in hospital, by lay people as well as by ministers. Catholics would expect to attend Mass every Sunday, on some feast days and sometimes daily. Orthodox Christians receive Communion from the time of their baptism in babyhood, but many Orthodox adults receive communion much less frequently than Roman Catholics or Anglicans. Non-conformists also take communion less often. The Salvation Army and the Quakers do not hold their own communion services but their members might choose to participate in those of other Christian churches. Jehovah's Witnesses commemorate the Lord's evening meal annually on the equivalent of Nisan 14 in the Jewish calendar.

CONFIRMATION

When a child who has been baptised is old enough to make its own promises to God, it may be brought for a service of Confirmation. This includes Roman Catholic, Anglican and Methodist Churches.

DEATH

Christians should be offered the help and support of the appropriate minister or chaplain at the time of death, or when a relative or friend is dying. It is the belief of Christians that the bodies of the dead should be treated with the same respect as if they were alive. There are usually no formal objections to post-mortems, transplants or body donations; it will depend on the individuals concerned. Families may wish to spend some time in prayer beside the bed of someone who has died. Some Christians choose to wear black as a sign of mourning. The sadness of death is seen against the background of hope in the Resurrection.

Latter-day Saints prefer burial to cremation and generally prefer to prepare their own members for burial. For Greek Catholic Christians, the corpse rests in an open coffin for three days. During the last night there is a watch at home by friends and family before the coffin is closed. Most coffins are taken to a service of Mass in a Church. After the Mass a Bible is put on the foot of the coffin and the congregation is asked to say their last farewells by kissing the Bible and walking clockwise around it. Then it is taken to the cemetery for a burial service. After 40 days there is another family service at the graveside.

DIET

There are no general dietary requirements, but some Christians prefer to eat no meat on Fridays. Some will abstain from food and drink before taking Holy Communion. Jehovah's Witnesses do not eat meat unless the blood has been properly drained away. Methodists traditionally do not drink alcohol, others take it in moderation. Drug-taking is frowned upon except for medical necessity. All Seventh-day Adventists, like Jews, are required to abstain from pork, shellfish and fish without fins or scales. Avoidance of tobacco and alcohol is advocated. Latter-day Saints (Mormons) do not drink alcohol, tea or coffee or use tobacco or other harmful drugs. They may also avoid meat, especially if it has blood in it.

DRESS

Generally speaking this is up to individuals concerned. Latter-day Saints dress modestly. Women usually wear full-length skirts and non-skimpy tops. Full members wear a special garment next to the skin. It should be treated with respect but may be removed for medical treatment and for activities like swimming. It would be part of burial clothing. Women within the Brethren tradition should not cut their hair and they should keep it covered.

EVANGELISM

Christians are called to share the good news of the gospel which Jesus taught, but they interpret this calling in different ways. Some Christians believe that they should strive to convert non-Christians; they may feel a commitment to go from house to house or to preach in public places. Other Christians, including Quakers and Unitarians, celebrate human and religious diversity and believe that people should be free to develop their spirituality in accordance with their conscience.

FAMILY LIFE

The family unit is very important and should provide a warm and loving environment for the nurturing of children within the faith. Latter-day Saints expect families to set aside an evening a week to play and study together. Many Churches put on services for families, especially at Christmas. Mothering Sunday is another traditional time for family services. Jehovah's Witnesses do not observe Christmas or birthdays as these are not based on Biblical tradition. Witnesses are more comfortable with the concept of spontaneous giving. They believe it is important to build up children's trust, to maintain moral standards of truth and integrity and to uphold scripture.

FASTING

During Lent, the 40 days of preparation for Easter, many people choose to observe some kind of fasting. This may mean moderating the diet or total abstinence for a period of time. Fasting is a recognised part of an Orthodox Christian's life. Wednesday and Friday each week, and a long period before Christmas and Easter have traditionally been times when no meat, fish, dairy products or alcohol were taken. In the Roman Catholic Church, Ash Wednesday and Good Friday are days when meat is avoided and only one main meal and two lighter snacks are taken. This does not apply to those under 7 or over 60, or to those who are sick. Latter-day Saints hold regular fast-days, usually on the first Sunday of each month during which neither food nor drink are taken. This is not expected of children, of the sick, or of women who are pregnant or breast-feeding.

FESTIVALS

Sunday has been celebrated since the beginning of Christianity as the day of Jesus' resurrection from the dead. Most Christians meet for worship on this day. Seventh-day Adventists, however, gather together on Saturdays, following the Jewish Sabbath tradition. They also try to honour the day by avoiding unnecessary work. The most important feast days are Christmas (25 Dec), celebrating the birth of Christ; Easter, remembering His death and resurrection; and Whitsun/ Pentecost, which celebrates the coming of God's Spirit, and the birth of the church. Most Orthodox Christians in Britain celebrate Christmas Day on 25 December, but some follow the Julian calendar and celebrate it on 7 January. The Orthodox Christians celebrate Easter (Pascha) on a date which is often considerably later then the western Easter. The western dates of Easter and Whitsun vary, as they are linked to old Pagan festivals of spring, and are based on a lunar calendar. There are many ancient symbols and customs associated with Christian festivals, some of which are also shared by people outside the Church.

LIFESTYLE

This varies from person to person, but there are some common characteristics. All Christians should follow the example of Jesus and his teaching which is highlighted in the Sermon on the Mount. Plymouth Brethren avoid many secular occupations, allowing only those compatible with the teaching of the New Testament. They also avoid leisure activities which bring them into contact with people and things which are deemed harmful. Exclusive Brethren would not watch TV, listen to the radio, read newspapers or fiction, use computers, the internet or mobile phones. Quakers avoid titles, preferring to be referred to or addressed simply by their Christian names.

MARRIAGE

Most Christians prefer to be married in church. Traditionally the bride wears white. Quaker weddings are a version of the usual Sunday meeting, adapted to meet the needs of the couple concerned. Since sharing and simplicity are emphasised wedding lunches will be modest affairs. Mixed faith marriages may be accepted within some churches. The status of same-sex partnerships is a matter of debate within some of the churches. Partnership blessings for same-sex relationships are offered increasingly by Unitarians. Exclusive Brethren are encouraged to marry early (within the faith) and have large families. Latter-day Saints do not permit sex before marriage or outside marriage; marriage should be between one man and one woman, and this union is solemnised in the temple for eternity. Most churches discourage if not forbid divorce, while extending understanding and support for individuals caught up in distressing family situations. Remarriage is acceptable within some Christian traditions. Christian marriages and blessings should reflect stable, loving and responsible relationships.

MEDICAL TREATMENT

There is generally no problem with most medical treatments. Abortion, simply to avoid the birth of an unwanted child, is unacceptable, except when the mother's life is at risk. There may be other exceptional circumstances, as in a case of rape. Fertility treatments involving the destruction of fertilised embryos are also likely to be rejected. In general, Christians do not view euthanasia as acceptable; nor do they feel that it is desirable to prolong treatment or life unnecessarily. Christian Scientists turn to God in the first instance when they are ill. They may seek the support of a Christian Science Practitioner (professional spiritual healer). They may also accept conventional medical treatment.

PASTORAL CARE AND SOCIAL CONCERN

Pastoral care is a very important aspect of Christian ministry. It is particularly important at times of stress. All Christians have the responsibility to show compassion and offer support to others, but at various moments in their lives Christians may want to see a minister or priest for guidance or confession. In hospitals, prisons, colleges or the armed services there are usually Christian chaplains on hand.

Those in hospital may welcome a visit from a chaplain or their own minister, especially before an operation. They may wish to visit the chapel, to attend a service or listen to it over the hospital radio. Prayer cards and Bibles should be available. In hospital some privacy would be needed when patients are receiving Holy Communion, or having a pastoral visit.

It is important to take seriously the pastoral needs of children. It is equally important to consider the pastoral and spiritual needs of the elderly, particularly if they are cut off from their regular support networks or are unable to continue with established and valued patterns of worship.

All the churches are committed to working within the wider community both in the UK and overseas. Christian Aid and CAFOD work with other partners throughout the world for the relief of poverty. The Salvation Army is the largest provider of Welfare Aid in the UK apart from the government.

PRAYER

The Lord's Prayer, taught by Jesus to his disciples, is treasured by Christians and used both in private and in public worship. (Our Father who art in heaven...)

RELIGIOUS SYMBOLS

Icons (sacred pictures of Christ, his Mother and the saints) are extremely important to Orthodox Christians. Religious statues, crucifixes and rosaries are important to Roman Catholics and Anglo-Catholics while some non-conformists may actually find them offensive.

WORSHIP

For some Churches, including Roman Catholic and Anglican, there are set forms of prayer and liturgy. Congregational worship is usually conducted by a priest. In non-conformist Churches like the Baptists, the worship is freer and there is more emphasis on the sermon. Ministers or elders lead the worship. Some Churches accept the leadership of women; others reject it as unscriptural. Charismatic congregations are found in most denominations.

The worship of the Roman Catholic Church centres on the Mass. The worship of the Orthodox Churches centres on the Divine Liturgy. By contrast, a Quaker Meeting is silent worship in the presence of the Spirit of God. There is nothing prearranged and no leader. No religious symbols are used and there are no rituals – no baptism, no eucharist, no anointing. Quakers sit together in mindful silence until somebody feels prompted to speak or read from the Bible or other literature. Everyone is welcome to join in Quaker meetings for Worship and anyone may feel the call to speak: man, woman, child, experienced Quaker or first time visitor.

HINDUS

The Hindu tradition has no founder and is best understood as a group of closely connected religious traditions, rather than a single religion, representing nevertheless a complete way of life. Hinduism can be traced back to at least 5000 BCE in the civilisations of the Indus Valley, from which the name is derived. It is inextricably bound up with culture and social structure. The teachings are enshrined within many holy books, including the Vedas, the Upanishads and the Srimad Bhagvat Geeta.

For many Hindus the numerous gods and goddesses of Hinduism are seen as aspects of the One divine principle, Brahman. The belief that there are many ways to worship Brahman leads to a tolerance of other religions.

At the heart of Hinduism is Dharma, the ancient law which underlies the order of the universe and is reflected in a moral and ethical life. Karma, the law of action and reaction, teaches humans how to behave, and shapes their destinies. Hindus consider that religion is a sanctified and disciplined path that one should follow to reach a higher goal, i.e. to become a better person.

Hindus believe in reincarnation, through myriad lives, until release is obtained. Reincarnation is bound up with the ancient Hindu principle of compassion for all living things. Release into divine bliss can be reached by human beings through the Way of Action, the Way of Knowledge, the Way of Devotion or the Way of Meditation.

Practices may vary considerably among Hindus, according to where they come from, according to caste, and according to personal preference. Although the caste system is not legally sanctioned in India, it still influences many people, and those from the traditionally higher castes may not wish to be touched by, or eat with, lower caste people.

ABLUTIONS AND HYGIENE

Some Hindus prefer washing in free flowing water and they would require water for washing to be available in the same room as the WC.

BIRTH

The birth of a baby is celebrated, especially the birth of the first boy. Soon after the birth it is customary for a close relative to be invited to put a drop of water and honey on the infant's tongue, celebrating the sweetness of life and the bond with the family. Mothers usually rest for about forty days after the birth and do not prepare food. Sometimes the baby's head is shaved at the 30th day. Sometimes the baby's name is kept a secret at first.

DEATH

After death the body should always be left covered. It is important to consult the family and ask if they wish to perform the last rites. It is traditional that female relatives wash the body of a dead woman; male relatives wash a dead man. Hindus are cremated. Usually the eldest son of the deceased takes a leading part in the ceremonies. Hindus may wish their ashes to be sprinkled in a holy river, such as the Ganges. Many carry Ganges water with them, and believe that it should be the last thing that is put into the mouth when a Hindu dies. White is the colour of mourning.

DIET

Hindus do not eat beef because cows are held to be sacred and they may find derogatory comments about cows offensive. Many Hindus are strict vegetarians and do not eat any sort of meat. They may also avoid eggs. Hindus would prefer not to use plates and utensils which have been used for non-vegetarian food. As for other vegetarians, food should be prepared and served separately from meat dishes. Some Hindus will only eat with their right hand, and may expect visitors to do the same.

DRESS

It is not generally acceptable for a girl or woman to have uncovered legs. Saris, or loose top and trousers are normal wear. The emphasis on modesty means that joining activities such as swimming may be problematic.

Gold jewellery worn next to the skin is believed by some Hindus to ward off diseases and these items will be removed reluctantly. Married women often wear a gold brooch given to them by their husbands, as well as gold bangles. Men of the highest caste (Brahmins) may wear a sacred thread over their right shoulder and around the body; it should only be removed if absolutely necessary.

FASTING

Very few Hindus would insist on fasting whilst in hospital, though they may practise this as part of their faith. Only the more devout Hindus, often women, are likely to fast. Sometimes fasting implies eating only 'pure' foods such as fruits or yoghurt, rather than complete abstinence.

FESTIVALS

Notable festivals are Holi (in the spring to mark the death of winter) and Diwali (in the autumn, celebrated with lamps and candles).

GREETINGS

When a younger Hindu greets an elder, the younger may touch the feet of the elder, as a mark of respect. When meeting with a family, or another group of Hindus, it is usual to begin by addressing greetings to the eldest member first.

Public displays of physical intimacy such as kissing and hugging are not the norm amongst Hindus.

IN A HINDU HOME

Most Hindu homes contain a small shrine to one of more gods. These will often feature a statue perhaps an aum symbol, candles and offerings of food or other gifts for the deity. It would be disrespectful to remove or handle things placed at the shrine.

When receiving a visitor it is considered polite to offer some food and drink and it could be seen as offensive for the visitor to refuse such offers.

MARRIAGE

Hindu marriage ceremonies can vary a great deal but the central focus is the sacred fire, around which the couple walks (5-7 times) while the priest reads aloud from the scriptures. A wedding can take place at any time of the year but the time of day is likely to be carefully chosen according to its astrological significance for the couple. Most Hindu marriages are arranged through the families. The pre-marriage celebrations last 3-5 days and involve all the relations. The bride usually goes to live with the bridegroom's family. Red and pink are considered to be auspicious colours to wear at a wedding ceremony.

MODESTY

Hindu women are likely to have a strong preference to be treated, examined and cared for by female professionals and should not be cared for in mixed wards except in emergency situations.

NAMES

Hindus may have several names – a personal name, a special name, and a family name.

WORSHIP

Hinduism is based on the community, rather than the congregation. The home is a place for devotion, but worship also takes place in the temple, or mandir. Visitors to a mandir will be expected to remove their shoes and cover their heads. They should also dress modestly. Seating is on the floor, and it is considered disrespectful to sit with feet pointing towards the sacred area at the front of the temple. Mandirs are only likely to be found in major cities.

Footnote:

Although Hinduism was originally an umbrella word covering the various beliefs and practices of the people of the Indus Valley, and strictly speaking only applies to Indian people, it has produced many gurus over the centuries and there are many movements emanating from or influenced by Hinduism which have attracted westerners into their ranks.

HUMANISTS

Humanism is an approach to life based on reason and our common humanity, and recognises moral values. It is founded on human nature and experience. The Humanist tradition has developed over thousands of years, in Eastern and Western civilisations, building on many complementary philosophies.

The defining characteristics of a Humanist are:

- no belief in any god, in an afterlife, or in anything supernatural
- the belief that we should all try to live full and happy lives, and help others to do the same
- the belief that all situations and people deserve to be judged on their own merits, by standards of reason and humanity
- the belief that individualism and social cooperation are equally important.

Humanists try to observe the golden rule: "Do not do to others what you would not like done to you."

Some Humanists would say they are atheists, while some prefer to describe themselves as agnostics – all live without religious or superstitious beliefs. A large section of the population is not religious, but would not say they were Humanist.

CELEBRATIONS

There are local celebrants, who are happy to arrange ceremonies to celebrate birth, marriage and death, appropriate for the individuals concerned.

DIET, TREATMENT, MODESTY ETC

There are no rules about any of these things for Humanists. They should be regarded as individuals, free to make their preference known.

FORM-FILLING

When filling in forms some people will want to say "none" or "I don't know" when asked what religion they are. Some may say "Humanist".

GREETING

There are no specific guidelines on this. Normally Humanists will adopt the convention of the country in which they live.

IN A HUMANIST HOME

You should show the same basic level of politeness and respect that you would wish shown in your own home. If individual Humanists have any 'house rules' (like not smoking indoors), then they should let visitors know.

HOSPITAL ETIQUETTE

When religious ceremonies are conducted for another patient you could either draw the curtains round the bed of the religious patient or ask if those not participating in the service in the ward would like their own curtains drawn.

HUMANIST VISITORS AND LOCAL CONTACTS

Just as religious patients may enjoy a visit from a chaplain or priest, non-religious patients, especially the terminally ill and their families, might like a visit from a Humanist hospital visitor.

JAINS

Jainism is an ancient religion originating in India. It has links with Buddhism and Hinduism but restrictions on foreign travel have limited its spread. Jains believe in an infinite universe with no beginning or end – there is no creator-God. A sage who has achieved enlightenment, is known as a "Jina", a "victorious one" which is the root of the name. Of its twenty-four sages, the latest is Mahavira, born c600BCE. Central to Jainist philosophy is the idea that all things, including objects such as stones, metal and earth, are alive and feeling. Therefore, Jains practise a strict code of ahimsa (non-violence) that permeates every aspect of life. Jainism is an ascetic religion, which emphasises the need to distance oneself from material cares, leading to the principle of aparigraha (non-possession/ renunciation).

ABLUTIONS

Jainism has no dogma, so each individual decides how much to adhere to the Jain code. Strict Jains, such as mendicants, often give up washing, in deference to the two main principles.of Jainism. The principle of renunciation teaches that the body is unclean, and that spiritual enlightenment can only be attained by austere detachment from material cares (such as hygiene or personal comfort). The principle of non-violence means that Jains avoid killing all creatures, including tiny bacteria on the body. They might also wish to avoid polluting water with the dirt from their bodies.

CHASTITY AND ABORTION

Intercourse is usually seen as a procreative function only. The principle of ahimsa means that abortion is not acceptable. Family planning as a means to reduce unnecessary suffering may be accepted by some.

CLOTHING

Jainism has adapted to the modern world and attitudes to clothing will vary, but the Jain code of purity and non-possession makes it likely that simple and practical clothes will be preferred. Leather is unlikely to be worn. Jain worshippers, especially Shvetambara monks, often wear a piece of cloth over their mouth to prevent them damaging the creatures that live in the air, and as a symbol of their dedication to purity in all things. Often a soft brush is carried to sweep insects away in their path, to avoid killing them.

COMPASSION

There is a strong element of personal responsibility in Jainism. Although there is such an emphasis on detachment, to allow people around you to suffer or cause others to suffer is considered contrary to the principle of ahimsa. Jains are often very active on the social and political fronts and are concerned and active on animal rights fronts. Family pets are common.

DEATH

Since Jains believe in an infinite universe, they subscribe to the theory of reincarnation, and believe that the state of one's karma will affect what happens to a person in the future. Jains believe that it is possible to escape the endless cycle of life and death through absolute detachment from worldly cares. Much emphasis is placed on self-purification i.e., salvation within oneself, through one's own actions. It is considered rare and precious to attain a human birth. Jains are cremated after their death.

DIET

Jains are usually strict vegetarians, although they may have adapted their diet to the modern world. Some are vegan. Jain monks, and others who wish to observe Jain principles rigorously, may avoid all foods that destroy life, such as root vegetables, or fruit with lots of seeds in it. Eggs, honey and alcohol are often avoided as well. All mendicants and some lay people only eat in daylight, to avoid hurting insects in the dark. Fasting, often protracted, is an integral element of Jainism, in line with the philosophy of renunciation. Salekhana, the act of fasting to death, is considered a holy way for advanced mendicants to choose to die. The craving of food is seen as the most material, base instinct that humans possess, tying us to a life of suffering, so ritual fasting represents an attempt to escape this.

EMPLOYMENT

Jains avoid violent professions, such as the meat-trade, or military careers. Even farming is considered destructive, since activities like ploughing the earth destroy minute creatures, and disrupt the earth itself. Manufacturing presents problems, since Jains believe metal and wood have feelings. Jains tend to engage in trade or become tertiary services providers, such as doctors, lawyers and accountants.

FESTIVALS

The holiest Jain festival is Paryushana-parva, the annual festival of confession, which takes place in August or September. The most important socially is Mahavira-jayanti, the celebration of the birthday of the Mahavira, which occurs in March or April. Both are attached to lunar cycles.

JEWS

The Jewish religion is one of the oldest of the monotheistic faiths. It is a total way of life, with a code of conduct which applies to every aspect of life from the cradle to the grave, from sunset to sunset.

The basic laws of Judaism are enshrined in the Torah (the first five books of Moses) and also in the Talmud, which is a vast collection of commentaries, expositions and interpretations. The Ten Commandments are embedded in the Torah.

ABLUTIONS

Jews are required to wash their hands before eating. In communities where a ritual bath exists, it is used for purification by men and women before the Sabbath, and by women before their wedding and after menstruation.

CIRCUMCISION

The circumcision and naming of Jewish boys (Brit Milah) takes place on the eighth day after birth. The ceremony is performed by a Jewish practitioner (mohel), and usually takes place in the home. It may be deferred if the baby is unwell. The name of a baby girl is announced by her father in the synagogue.

COMING OF AGE

Jewish boys are Bar Mitzvah at the age of 13, when they take their full part with other men in the life of the synagogue. Girls are Bat-Mitzvah at 12 years.

DEATH

Euthanasia is forbidden. A Jewish patient who is dying may wish to hear the Shema (Hear O Israel, the Lord your God is one God...), or the 23rd Psalm (The Lord is my Shepherd...). Traditionally someone who is dying should not be left alone, and relatives are likely to sit with the dying person during the last hours or days. The Chevra Kadisha, Jewish Burial Society, should be notified and it will take care of all the arrangements. Autopsy is not generally acceptable. The funeral should normally take place within 24 hours, though the body cannot be moved on the Sabbath. Cremation is not generally acceptable. Flowers are not usually sent. Simplicity rather than show is stressed at Jewish funerals. Generally mourners do not wear black or buy new clothes for the occasion.

There may be open displays of grief at the funeral. Close relatives are likely to help to shovel the earth onto the coffin and other mourners can follow suit. A mourning period of seven days takes place for family members, during which they will not be expected to work.

Jews do not emphasise a belief in the afterlife, preferring to live well in this life, leaving the rest in God's hands.

DIET

Most Jews will require kosher food, specially prepared under supervision. Jews will not eat pork in any form. Among other forbidden foods are rabbit, shellfish, crustacea and fish without fins and scales. Most Jews will accept a vegetarian diet in hospital or in another home. Observant Jews obey the rule that says meat and milk products may not be eaten together at the same meal. During Passover unleavened bread must be eaten, precluding most cakes and wheat-based foods. Other special foods may be required.

DRESS

Orthodox Jewish men keep their heads covered all the time, and all Jewish men do so in the synagogue. Orthodox women also keep their heads covered and some will wear a wig. Some will not wear trousers or sleeveless tops. Liberal Jews may not be distinguishable by any dress code. Some observant Jews wear a beard and may also have side-locks. During various periods in the religious calendar, some Jews will not shave at all.

FASTING

The main fast of the year occurs in the autumn on Yom Kippur (Day of Atonement). It is a total fast lasting 25 hours, though medical advice will be respected if fasting is considered harmful to health. Religious Jews also observe other fast days. Young children, pregnant and nursing women, diabetics and the sick are not expected to fast.

FESTIVALS

The Jewish calendar is a lunar calendar, and so festival dates vary from year to year when compared with the secular calendar. Among the most important festivals are Rosh Hashanah, which is the New Year, and Sukkot, the Autumn Feast of Tabernacles. Another is Pesach, or Passover, celebrated in the spring and commemorating the Exodus of the Jews from Egypt. In preparation for the Passover, the house is thoroughly spring-cleaned and all traces of leaven are removed. It is important for families to gather together for the major festivals, which like the Sabbath begin at sunset and end an hour after sunset.

GREETING

There are no fixed forms of greeting. Orthodox Jews would not expect overly physical displays of affection between those of the opposite sex. A very Orthodox Jew will not touch any woman other than his wife and immediate family.

IN A JEWISH HOME

A Jewish home can be identified by a mezuzah, a small ornamental case fixed to the right hand doorpost by the front door. It contains the Shema, the central prayer.

MARRIAGE AND FAMILY LIFE

According to Orthodox Jews, a Jew is a person whose mother is Jewish. For Progressive "Liberal" Jews, a person is accepted as Jewish if either of their parents is Jewish. Judaism is a family-centred faith and the home is the centre of Jewish life. The weekly Sabbath sustains and strengthens family life.

A wedding is a time for great festivity. A rabbi conducts the marriage ceremony. The couple make their vows under a canopy.

Divorce is acceptable in certain circumstances.

MODESTY

Jews usually dress in a modest manner, and prefer to remain suitably clothed, even in a hospital bed. Mixed-sex wards are not acceptable. There is usually no objection to doctors or nurses of either sex.

SABBATH

The Sabbath (seventh day) is the last day of the Jewish week. It begins on Friday at sunset and ends one hour after sunset on Saturday. The beginning of the Sabbath on Friday evening is celebrated by the family with special prayers, rituals and food. The Mother lights the Sabbath candles and recites a blessing. Sabbath observance takes the form of prayer and contemplation, therefore no work is carried out, no money is spent and only travel on foot is permitted. It is important to remember that some Jews interpret the 'day of rest' rule strictly, and some will not even use a phone on the Sabbath.

WORSHIP

Visitors to a synagogue will be expected to dress modestly, with arms and legs covered, and women wearing a skirt or dress, rather than trousers. They may also be expected to cover their heads. In some synagogues, men and women sit separately.

MUSLIMS

Islam is an Arabic word meaning "submission" or "surrender". The word originally derived from the word "salaam", which means to be at perfect peace. Its full connotation is, therefore, "the perfect peace which comes when one's life is totally submitted to God." Islam, based on the Oneness of God, emphasises divine mercy and forgiveness.

Allah (meaning 'the God') is the Originator of all that exists and thus the Creator of the world and of man. Islam is the religion of every prophet of Allah from Adam through to Muhammad among whom are included Noah, Abraham, Moses and Jesus (peace be upon them). All brought the same message of the unity of God and called for submission to His will. The prophet Muhammad (peace be upon him) was not the founder of Islam, but rather the last prophet and messenger of Allah. He brought the final revelation, the Qur'an, in the 7th century CE.

ABLUTIONS AND HYGIENE

Muslims have to observe certain rules of cleanliness and prefer water for washing in the same room as the WC. They prefer to wash in free-flowing water and need shower facilities. Ablutions are performed before each prayer-time. After menstruation women are required to take a full bath or shower. Personal cleanliness is very important to Muslims and understood to be part of faith. Muslim adults are required to take a bath at least once a week and generally shave their armpits and pubes.

BIRTH

Abortion is unacceptable, except in extreme circumstances, as when the mother's life is in danger. It should be performed before the sixteenth week of pregnancy.

It is Muslim custom to make the Adhan (pronounced "azan"), the call to prayer, at the moment a child is born, so that these words "there is no deity worthy of worship except Allah" are the first words the child hears. Any Muslim may perform this task, though it is usually done by the father. Where possible only female maternity staff should be present during child birth. It is important that maternity staff know about these customs and facilitate them. In cases of miscarriage or stillbirth there may be a funeral ceremony. Some Muslims may wish to bury the placenta.

CIRCUMCISION

In Islam, circumcision of boys is required, and it is usually performed at an early age, preferably on the 7th day. Some clarification on whether the hospital will perform the operation is required, as the parents may ask for it to be done before the child leaves hospital. Information should be on hand about what facilities are available.

DEATH

The patient's face should, if possible, be turned towards Makkah, Saudi Arabia (South East) and a relative or another Muslim should be summoned to whisper in Arabic in the ear of the Muslim the article of the faith "there is no deity worthy of worship but Allah". These should be the last words heard by the dying person. If possible Muslims may also recite the Qur'an audibly near the patient.

The body should be handled with care and it should not be uncovered, except for washing. The body should be washed by people of the same sex. There are set prayers which follow a death and these are preferably said at the mosque. For Muslims it is required that the body be buried as soon as possible. A post-mortem should be avoided if legally possible and the body should be released quickly to the relatives. It is customary amongst some cultures for the bereaved to express their emotion freely when a relative has died; therefore privacy should be provided. Cremation is prohibited. Islam states that the body belongs to God and all of it should be buried. Therefore no part of it should be cut out or harmed although Muslims differ about donation. Therefore autopsy is prohibited except on sound medical or judicial grounds. Euthanasia is forbidden.

Since Muslim funerals are plain, donations to charities are preferred to flowers. Widows from some cultural backgrounds may stay indoors for 130 days after the funeral.

DIET

Pork and anything containing pork, cooked near pork, or processed using pork extracts is forbidden. This includes lard, gelatine and some cheeses. Animals must be killed in the right way, by a Muslim, and with prayer. Some Muslims consider shellfish, apart from prawns, and fish without scales as prohibited. Muslims do not eat carnivorous animals or anything that feeds on dirt or blood. Acceptable food is called "halal" and forbidden food is "haram". Jewish kosher food would be acceptable to Muslims. Any food and drink containing alcohol is forbidden. Alcohol is, however, permissible as a constituent of medication, if there is no other alternative. All halal food should be prepared, cooked and served separately to other food.

FASTING

During the month of Ramadan a Muslim does not eat or drink (even water) between sunrise and sunset (between the first prayer and the fourth prayer of the day). Fasting is excused for women during menstruation, pregnancy, after recent childbirth, or when breast-feeding; it is excused for all who are very old or young, sick or on a journey. It should be noted that fasting may be interpreted as not accepting anything into the body in any way, including medication by injection.

FESTIVALS

The major festivals are Eid-ul-Fitr, which brings Ramadan to an end, and Eid-ul-Adha, which marks the end of the time of the pilgrimage to Makkah (Haj). These are important times for families to be together.

FIVE PILLARS

The five pillars of Islam are the tenets and practices essential to the faith. These are: the proclamation that God is One and Muhammad is his prophet (Shahadah), offering prayer 5 times a day (Salat), almsgiving (Zakat), fasting during Ramadan (Saum), and undertaking a pilgrimage to Mecca (Haj) at least once in a lifetime, if it is possible.

GREETINGS

When two Muslims greet each other they might say "Assalamu Alaikum" (peace be upon you). Modesty discourages physical forms of greeting (kissing, hugging etc.), between members of the opposite sex, unless they are related. For some Muslim communities, shaking hands is acceptable, even between members of the opposite sex. In some Islamic countries, such as Morocco, young men may have close friendships and hold hands in public, but this practice is cultural rather than Islamic.

IN A MUSLIM HOME

You might see a copy of the Qur'an in pride of place, and you might also see prayer mats ready for use. You should offer to remove shoes when entering a Muslim home.

MARRIAGE

There is no set form of marriage, as Muslims come from many different cultural backgrounds. Normally speaking Muslims marry partners from within their own faith, but both bride and groom should give their consent. Normally a bride's guardian has to consent too. Under exceptional circumstances a man may marry up to 4 wives with their express consent as long as he treats them all equally. Under Islamic law, divorce is allowed, but discouraged.

Pregnancy outside marriage is considered a cardinal sin. Cohabitation and adultery are likewise forbidden.

MEDICINE

Islam has made major contributions to the study of medicine and doctors are highly respected.

Muslims from some cultural backgrounds would not expect to have medical information discussed directly with the patient, preferring to refer the matter to male relatives, including uncles and cousins.

MODESTY

Men and women are required to dress and behave modestly. Some Muslim women prefer to keep their hair (and neck) covered in public at all times. In Islam free mixing of sexes is not encouraged and this is sometimes interpreted quite strictly. If it is necessary to speak to a Muslim woman, it may be necessary for other family members, including children, to be present. Muslims should not be accommodated in mixed wards except in an emergency. Generally Muslims prefer to be examined by medical staff of the same sex. It is always preferable to have female professionals to care for women.

MOSQUE

Visitors to a mosque will be expected to dress modestly, with legs and arms covered. Women should have their heads covered too, and are asked to avoid visiting a mosque when they are menstruating. Shoes are removed before entering a mosque. Women and men sit separately in a mosque. Seating is on the floor, and care ought to be taken not to point the feet towards the 'Qibla' (the wall niche which shows the direction of Makkah – the direction Muslims face when praying). Music and raising one's voice in the mosque is forbidden.

PRAYER

Muslims are required to pray five times a day at set times, according to the positions of the sun. They face towards Makkah and prostrate themselves to pray. Women who are menstruating, or who have post-natal bleeding are not required to do this. Muslims physically unable to stand may make their prayer sitting, or lying down. Shoes are removed and heads usually covered before prayer. Muslims are required to pray in a clean area with clean clothes. Urine and excrement in an area or on clothes will have to be cleaned first before obligatory prayer. Adult males are highly encouraged to take part in special prayers on Fridays which includes a sermon.

PAGANS

Paganism is a name for the nature-based religions, found all over the world including Shintoism in Japan and the native religions of America, Australasia and Africa. There are also many Pagans in the UK, following the polytheistic and/or pantheistic religions of pre-Christian times in ways appropriate to modern life.

The word "pagan" means "peasant", after the country people who first practised this way of life. Pagans see the divine in everything around them, especially in nature. Each tree, rock, river and creature is believed to have a spirit. Therefore the sanctity of life is important to Pagans. Pagans also emphasise environmental concerns.

The beliefs about gods are varied in Paganism. Some Pagans believe in many gods and goddesses, whilst others see them as symbols that help them to understand the world. Pagans believe that divine forces can be seen in terms of male and female, and can be found and approached both within and without one's self. Pagan traditions tend to stress the importance of the female, especially in the face of patriarchal society.

Pagans have no founding father or holy book, but derive their teachings from a variety of sources, including ancient mythology and a study of nature. Therefore Pagan groups tend to see all morality as being relative to the situation. It is the individual's responsibility to make ethical choices for themselves, whilst trying to live compassionate lives.

There are many Pagans around, but because of misunderstanding about their beliefs they sometimes choose to be anonymous. For example, Pagans do not believe in a devil.

There are many different branches within Paganism, such as Heathenry, Druidism, Wicca and Shamanism. Pagans have no churches, but a network of small inter-related traditions. Some also make use of the large national contact groups, such as the Pagan Federation. Some Pagans will want to give you the name of their spiritual adviser, who can give you guidance about their needs.

CHILDREN AND CONVERSION

Since Pagans stress the importance of personal freedom, they think people should choose their own spiritual path. Therefore the children of Pagans are allowed to decide for themselves. Proselytising (by Pagans and non-Pagans alike) is regarded as inappropriate and ill-mannered.

DEATH

Many Pagans allow the corpse to "rest" for three nights before the funeral, to allow the soul to depart. The corpse is normally kept at home for the wake. Pagans usually have no objections to autopsies, if they are considered necessary. Allowing the body to rest inviolate for three nights will obviously render organs useless for donation. However, the choice to donate body parts is an individual one and each Pagan should make their wishes known on this subject well in advance.

In cases of terminal illness, Pagans prefer a natural death with dignity to being kept alive indefinitely by drugs. Such a death is preferred to take place at home, with friends and loved ones. Doctors should not try to extend the life of a Pagan patient who would prefer to die at home.

Most Pagans believe in reincarnation.

DIET

Many Pagans are vegetarian, but this is an individual choice and hospital authorities would be automatically informed upon admission. As a central element of many Pagan celebrations is drinking ale or wine and eating bread, attention must be given to "nil by mouth" advice. Those pagans who eat meat would be concerned that the animals had been reared kindly and killed humanely.

FESTIVALS

Pagans celebrate a variety of festivals, depending upon their tradition. Usually these are based around agricultural, solar or lunar tides. In hospital, their main requirement will be privacy, and advice on arranging a time free of ward rounds to observe the festival. The different Pagan traditions celebrate different festivals, but some, particularly Wiccans, celebrate these: Imbolc (Feb 2), Eostre at the Spring Equinox (Mar 21), Beltane (May 1), the Midsummer Solstice (Jun 21/2), Lammas at the Harvest Season (Aug 2), the Autumn Equinox (Sep 21), Samhain (Oct 31), Yule at the Winter Solstice (Dec 21/2). Festivals are often observed on the night leading up to the day concerned (e.g. for Beltane, sunset on 30 April to sunrise on May 1).

GREETING

There are no formal styles of greeting, though Pagans generally tend to be physically demonstrative with each other.

IN A PAGAN HOME

One might expect to see statuary of various gods, connected back to those cultures to which the individual Pagan is drawn (Ancient Egypt, Greece, the Heathen Tribelands, Ancient Britain etc.) Pictures and iconography are very common too, and various shrines or altars to different deities might be seen around the house. Sometimes the icons and statues may have a strongly erotic element, which could surprise some visitors. For a visitor to handle religious items would be inappropriate, but the householder will probably be happy to answer any questions as to the nature of items. Pets are a common feature of Pagan homes.

MARRIAGE

The Pagan marriage ceremony is called a hand-fasting. The usual form is this: initially Pagans marry for a year and a day, at the end of which time they can renew their vows. Paganism is fully accepting of same-sex marriages. Though such marriages are not recognised in law (except in Scotland), the rights of the marital partner to be with their spouse should be acknowledged.

MEDICINE

Homeopathic and other such remedies are commonly used by Pagans. Patients will make doctors aware of any such remedies that they are taking and these should be integrated with mainstream treatments, not denigrated or rejected. Some Pagan patients may wish to be attended by a spiritual healer while in hospital. Such healings could take place within a quiet room, or more simply by drawing the curtains round the bed to give privacy both to the Pagan and to other patients.

Pagans believe in a spirit-world, and often feel that some psychoactive drugs can disturb their interactions with that world. Except in the case of emergencies, doctors should always make clear to the patient any psychoactive side effects of medication before drugs are administered. The patient must then be allowed the right to refuse medication if the side-effects are considered undesirable. A Pagan patient who reports seeing spirits (perhaps the soul of a dead relative, or some form of nature spirit) is not necessarily exhibiting signs of mental disturbance or distress, nor having a bad drug-reaction. Within Paganism such spiritual visions are considered quite normal, and even desirable.

SYMBOLS

Many Pagans use ritual weapons, such as a knife (known as an athame) in their personal worship. Such are kept for purely symbolic purposes but may cause some concern over security. In hospital this can be got round by the provision of a secure bedside locker. There may be talismans and objects of reverence which Pagan patients wish to wear. The pentagram is a well-known Pagan symbol, representing the five elements of earth, air, fire, water and spirit. Please behave sensitively when requesting a Pagan to remove jewellery.

WORSHIP

Pagans prefer to worship out of doors, communing with nature in a peaceful outdoor setting. Where hospitals have a garden area, the patient should be made aware of its existence and allowed visits, where illness permits.

Pagan worship seeks to honour the divine powers and to bring the participants in harmony with them, to celebrate the turning of the seasons, and to mark the transitions of human life with appropriate rites of passage. Rituals usually begin with the marking of sacred space. They may involve meditation, chanting, music, prayer, dance, poetry, drama and the sharing of food and drink.

Part of some Pagan traditions is the performance of monthly ceremonies based round the lunar cycle. These rituals are performed during the hours of darkness, which may cause some conflict with hospital desires for regimented curfews. With tactful negotiations, both parties can come to a mutual agreement.

RASTAFARIANS

Rastafarianism was formulated amongst the dispossessed black population in Jamaica in the early 20th century. A variety of movements grew that sought to emphasise the dignity and pride of black inheritance and promised the possibility of African political and economic independence. Rastafarianism is thus a movement of people who are struggling to reclaim their African ancestry by identifying with African cultures and traditions, including elements of the Shango religion from West Africa.

Marcus Garvey was a prominent figure within Rastafarianism who prophesied the crowning of a black king in Africa. Rastafarians believe this prophecy was fulfilled when Haile Selassie was crowned first of all King, and later Emperor, of Ethiopia in 1930. Haile Selassie was known as Ras (Prince) Tafari, hence the name of his followers. He is seen as being the direct descendant of kings David and Solomon, and is called 'Jah', or the living manifestation of God.

Rastafarianism is a way of life rather than an organised religion, and is guided by the concept of peace and love. Distrusting official hierarchy, the majority of Rastas are not affiliated to a particular group. However, the Ethiopian Church is seen as their spiritual home.

The Bible is seen as the divine Word. It is interpreted by Rastafarians through collective reading, study and debate, which is known amongst Rastafarians as 'reasoning'. Rastafarians particularly emphasise the Old Testament and the Book of Revelation.

Rastas prefer the term 'principles', rather than 'beliefs', holding that the latter implies doubt. Central principles are that God, Jesus, the Israelites and early Christians were black and that Christians misrepresent Jesus as a blue-eyed European; Rastafarians are true Jews; the Bible is authoritative and was written by and for black people; black people will only be free when they are back in Africa.

It is important to recognise the diversity within the faith, which is open to all members of society, black or white. Therefore the individual must be consulted, especially before medical treatment, as some may follow Old Testament laws more strictly than others.

BIRTH

Most Rastafarians oppose contraception. Abortion is not usually considered acceptable. African traditions connected with the disposal of the placenta and umbilical cord may need to be observed. After giving birth the woman is considered unclean. Whilst in aftercare, Rastafarian Sisters need to have free flowing water close at hand.

CLEANLINESS

During her menstrual period a woman is considered unclean and requires free flowing water. The same applies to men who are being treated for venereal diseases, or have a discharge.

Hair has much significance to Rastafarians. Uncut, matted hair in locks, known as dreadlocks, are common, especially amongst male Rastafarians. Dreadlocks are seen as a symbol of strength, representing breaking away from the 'Babylonian' system of western society. The uncut locks also represent the mane of the lion, the symbol of African strength and emancipation. Therefore, a Rasta's hair should be treated with respect, and all cutting of it should be avoided. Dreadlocks are often cleaned with olive or coconut oil. Frequently, beards are also left uncut.

CLOTHING AND MODESTY

Some Rastafarians will wish to cover their hair, often with a hat (called a tam) bearing the four colours of especial importance to their faith. These colours are black, red, green and gold/yellow, which stand respectively for: the black race; the blood of slavery; the promised land; and a golden future. Rastafarians often have other items with these colours too. All items bearing these four colours should be treated with respect.

Women are encouraged to dress modestly, and to refrain from wearing trousers or make-up. Sometimes Rastafarians, particularly women, will be unwilling to wear garments that have been worn by non-Rastafarian people. Disposable theatre gowns may therefore be preferred in hospital.

DEATH

'Dead' and 'death' are words considered negative and are rarely used by Rastafarians, who follow the more positive concept of 'ever-living'. 'Passed' or 'passing' are terms often used, reinforcing the Rastafarian belief that life is eternal through the spirit. Some Rastas believe in reincarnation.

There are no religious rituals. No priest is required. If he is available the local head of the 'Twelve Tribes' may be sent for. Rastafarians have no objection to cremation but prefer burial. The 'Nazarite Vow', a principle adhered to by Rastas, enjoins the shunning of dead bodies, which may be prepared for burial by family members, or preferably an undertaker. Attendance at funerals is not emphasised, as Rastafarianism celebrates life, rather than death.

DIET

Rastafarians often have a strong emphasis on living in harmony with the natural world, and accordingly most are vegetarians and some are vegans. Pork and pork products are banned. Fish must have fins and scales. The term used as a model for the ideal diet is 'Ital', meaning a saltless, vegetarian diet. 'Ital' also means natural food. Sometimes this is extended to include all canned or chemical food. Many Rastafarians abstain from alcohol and tobacco, although the use of cannabis is seen as being sanctioned by the Bible. This may need to be taken into consideration by health professionals when administering medicine.

FASTS AND FESTIVALS

Rastafarians are required to fast and may choose to do this on Saturday, the Jewish Sabbath. It is important to consult the individual to assess their fasting habits. July 23 is the birthday of Haile Selassie, this is one of the major festivals of the year. November 2 is Haile Selassie's Coronation celebration. During October the Organisation of African Unity celebrates African Culture. The year's highlight is 7th January which is the Ethiopian Christmas. It is popularly known as Rasmus. Birthdays are not widely celebrated.

IN A RASTAFARIAN HOME

You might well see a picture of Haile Selassie, along with a copy of the Bible. The lion is also a Rastafarian symbol. There are often items in black, red, green and yellow. There may also be a flag, usually Jamaican or Ethiopian. Visitors may be asked to remove their shoes.

MARRIAGE

Because of their distrust of formal procedures, there is no formal system of marriage within Rastafarianism. Marriage is looked upon as part of the establishment and is not, therefore, encouraged, but commitment to a partner is encouraged and sexual permissiveness is banned. A man and woman who cohabit are automatically viewed as husband and wife. A couple need stay together only for as long as both desire it.

MEDICAL TREATMENT

Generally speaking, Rastas are distrustful towards western medicines and would often prefer alternative treatments such as herbalism, homeopathy and acupuncture.

Rastafarians are completely against any pig product, which includes transgenic hearts, kidneys and heart valves. It is permissible to accept transfusions and blood from family members. However, some will not accept blood transfusion, and some will. It is important to consult individuals. Rastafarians do not carry donor cards and are against any scientific use of the body after death. Prolonging life is considered unacceptable when the person remains in a vegetative state after every attempt has been made to help. Medicines that have damaging side effects should not be used. The use of marijuana to relieve pain would be preferred.

WORSHIP

As Rastafarianism is not an organised religion, there does not tend to be a specific place of worship. Some communities will hold weekly meetings in a community centre or in a private house. These meetings include worship, the discussion of community matters and music. Women must cover their heads at these meetings.

SIKHS

A Sikh believes in one God, and follows the teachings of the ten Gurus as contained in the Guru Granth Sahib (the Sikh Holy Book). The Guru Granth Sahib also contains the verses of bhagats (devotees) teaching similar ideas, including Muslims and Hindus. The Guru Granth Sahib is found in every Gurdwara (door to the Guru) and is treated with veneration as the Word of God. The ultimate Guru (teacher) is God, who is often referred to as Vahiguru (wonderful teacher). The first Guru, Guru Nanak Dev, was born in 1469 in the Punjab, in north-west India. The mother tongue of Sikhs is Punjabi.

Sikhs are now living all over the world, thriving in many different cultural contexts. There will be variations in practice but they will share the same basic principles. Guru Nanak taught equality, and emphasised social mobility and universal brotherhood in a situation where Muslims and Hindus were strictly divided. This is reflected in the fact that although Sikhs meet together for worship in the Gurdwara, their community life also centres on the langar (community kitchen), where all are welcome and all can be fed, irrespective of faith and culture. A central tenet of Sikhism is to serve God by living a truthful and upright life in the service of others.

ABLUTIONS AND HYGIENE
Personal cleanliness is important. Water for washing should be provided in the same room as the WC. Showers are preferable to a bath, though a jug and basin may be used instead. Initiated Sikhs should get up and bathe (shower) before reading their morning prayers.

DEATH
The body is washed and new clothes put on it before cremation. Sons and other male members of the family attend to the father's body and daughters and other females prepare the mother's body. The 5 'K's'* (see below) should not be removed. If the patient's Kachhera have to be removed, they should be replaced with another pair. White is the colour of mourning. Sikh funerals are very simple and no memorials are allowed. Death is not seen as final in the cycle of birth and death, merely as a stage in the transmigration of the soul. Sikhs believe that the soul travels through a number of existences until eventually the soul merges in the All-Soul (God) like a drop of water merges in the ocean. The human body is the last rung on the ladder of reincarnation.

DIET
Initiated Sikhs should not take any intoxicants (alcohol, tobacco, recreational drugs). Most initiated Sikhs are strict vegetarians: no meat, no fish, no eggs. Sikhs in general do not eat beef; some choose to eat other meats, especially chicken. It is very important to check each person's individual requirements.

FAMILY LIFE

Most Sikhs come from South Asia and follow South Asian traditions (see South Asian chapter), with close family ties and respect for the older generation.

FASTING

There are no universal fasting requirements. In fact, the Guru Granth Sahib speaks out against any type of fasting, and also against over indulgence. (Some Sikh women may choose to abstain from salt on the day of the full moon, but this is for cultural rather than for religious reasons.)

FESTIVALS

Sikhs celebrate "gurpurbs" which are dates related to the lives of the ten Sikh Gurus, and dates connected to the Guru Granth Sahib, which after Guru Gobind Singh became the eternal Guru of the Sikhs. On these occasions a full reading of the Guru Granth Sahib takes place, lasting three days.

The two main events in the Sikh calendar are the birthday of the first Guru, Guru Nanak, in November and Vaisakhi, celebrated around April 13, commemorating the creation of the order of the Khalsa (the community of the pure) by Guru Gobind Singh. Vaisakhi is also the Sikh New Year. New members are initiated (take Amrit), there is an Akhand Parth, the Nishan Sahib is replaced by a new flag; there is hymn singing, preaching, various festivities, dancing and competitions.

When Hindus celebrate Diwali (festival of lights), Sikhs commemorate the release of the sixth Guru, Guru Hargobind, from prison along with 52 Hindu princes. He was offered his freedom by the Moghul authorities, but refused to leave unless his 52 fellow political prisoners were also set free.

FIVE K's

These items have great religious and spiritual significance and are compulsory attire for initiated Sikhs, both men and women. Other Sikhs may wear some of them.

Kesh	hair, no cutting, trimming or shaving of hair anywhere on the body. (Do not throw away hair from combs with rubbish). Uncut hair is a symbol of spirituality, showing acceptance of God's will.
Kangha	comb. This is a symbol of cleanliness and orderliness.
Karah	steel bracelet. This is a reminder of the unity and omnipresence of God, and the need for restraint.
Kachhera	special unisex shorts/ underwear. They symbolise chastity and self-control. (They were originally worn by people working in the fields to preserve modesty.)
Kirpaan	sword (ornamental, usually very small). It symbolises dignity, and the Sikh struggle against injustice.

GREETING

As with people from most parts of South Asia, Sikh men and women do not usually touch each other when greeting. Many Sikhs greet each other by putting their hands together and bowing, in respect for the divine in the other person. People of the same gender do touch, shake hands and even hug. Sikh greetings are: Sat Sri Akal (the Timeless One is True) and Vahiguru Ji Ka Khalsa, Vahiguru Ji Ki Fateh (the Khalsa is with God, the victory is with God). When meeting a group of Sikhs it would be normal to begin by greeting the eldest first. There is no objection to shaking hands.

HEAD COVERING

Most Sikh men and some women cover their heads with a turban. It should be treated with great respect. Women may veil their heads, particularly in the Gurdwara. Children may also cover their heads. Sikh head coverings have spiritual significance. Some Sikhs have broken with the tradition of long hair and head coverings for various reasons, including difficulties in the past with employers. They may be very sensitive about this.

IN A SIKH HOME

On entering a Sikh home you should offer to remove your shoes. Some families keep the Guru Granth Sahib in a special prayer room. That room has then become a Gurdwara and should be treated as such by visitors. It is customary to offer refreshments to guests and it might be seen as impolite to refuse them.

MARRIAGE

Sikh marriages are likely to be arranged by the families concerned. There are about two weeks of celebrations before the event. The actual ceremony is centred on the scriptures. As the granthi (reader) reads set stanzas from the Guru Granth Sahib the bride and groom walk round it four times. The bride and groom often make their home with the bridegroom's family.

MEDICAL TREATMENT

Sikhs are permitted to take prescribed medicine. Abortion is not generally considered acceptable.

MODESTY

Sikh families have strong traditions about modesty. Sikh women usually wear a salwar or pajamis, and tend to have their arms covered. Sikh women who wear western style clothes prefer trousers to skirts. Some women veil their faces in the presence of men who are older than their husbands, but this is a cultural variation and not a Sikh requirement. Female patients generally prefer to be attended by female doctors. Sikh women should not be accommodated in mixed wards except in emergencies.

NAMES

The tenth Sikh Guru, Guru Gobind Singh, ordained that all Sikh men should be called Singh and all Sikh women should be called Kaur. This is to show that they are all equal. First names are unisex. The mother takes the new baby to the Gurdwara for the normal service and the Granthi (reader) opens the Guru Granth Sahib at random and takes the first letter of the first stanza as a guide to the baby's name, which is then announced to the congregation. Some Asians have westernised their names.

PRINCIPLES

Sikhs believe that an individual should make every effort to overcome anger, greed, pride and passion, and should work hard to earn a decent living. Sikhs recognise three levels of service: physical service, which is being of assistance to those who require help; mental service, which involves enlightening others about God and righteousness; material service, in the form of financial contributions to noble causes. Sikhs are very tolerant of the view of others, seeing all as friends and respecting people of different faiths.

WORSHIP

A devout Sikh will rise very early, bathe and then spend some time in meditation before saying the morning set prayers. There are also evening prayers. These prayers may be said privately, or with the family. In the UK it is usual for the collective worship to be on a Sunday.

Sikhs worship together in the gurdwara, but a gurdwara is a centre for educational, social and welfare activities as well as a place for communal worship.

At the gurdwara visitors will be expected to dress modestly, with legs and head covered. Shoes are removed. Visitors are asked not to bring tobacco products into the gurdwara. Seating is on the floor. Sometimes men and women sit separately. Care should be taken to avoid pointing one's feet towards the dais on which the holy text, the Guru Granth Sahib, sits. At the end of the service, kara prashad, a holy food, is given to the worshippers. The service is followed by a shared meal in the langar (community kitchen/dining hall).

SOUTH ASIANS

The term 'South Asian' is a loose term generally applied to people from the Indian subcontinent – i.e. those from India, Pakistan, Bangladesh, Nepal and Sri Lanka. This land mass is larger than the size of Europe, and contains many different cultures, religions, languages and ethnicities. There are, however, some common cultural beliefs.

In India around 85% of the population are Hindus and 10% are Muslims. Prominent also are Sikhs, Christians, Buddhists, Jains, Jews and Parsees (Zoroastrians). Most Sikhs are from the province called the Punjab. In the UK the biggest regional groups amongst Indian Hindus, Sikhs and Christians are the Punjabis and the Gujaratis. There are 17 major languages in India, and over 500 dialects. The most commonly spoken languages are Hindi, Urdu, Punjabi, Gujarati, Bengali and English.

Pakistan is an Islamic state, which means nearly all Pakistanis are Muslim. The main language spoken is Urdu, although Sindhi, Pashto and Punjabi also feature prominently. India and Pakistan each have a state called Punjab, since the original Punjab region was divided when Pakistan was created in the Partition of India in 1947.

Bangladesh is only two thirds of the size of the UK, but has twice the population – it is therefore one of the most densely populated countries in the world. Most Bangladeshis are Sunni Muslims.

It is important to recognise that not only are there differences in culture within South Asian groups, but that other factors will influence behaviour. For example, attitudes in urban areas are often different to those in rural areas. Migrants to other countries may adapt to the majority culture, and thus put less emphasis on tradition; alternatively they may adhere to traditions in a more rigid fashion than those in the country of origin, who feel no threat to their culture and so can adapt with the times.

DIET

Diet will vary according to region, religion and custom. Many South Asians, especially Hindus, Buddhists and Sikhs, follow a strictly vegetarian diet, eating neither meat nor meat derivatives. Some will also avoid eggs and root vegetables. Hindus do not eat beef. Muslims do not eat pork, and only eat meat that is halal, i.e. has been killed according to Islamic law. Many South Asians eat only with their right hand, since the difficulty in obtaining clean water has made it a custom to designate the left hand as having a separate toilet facility. Historically, those who ate with their left hands were more likely to be diseased, and so were shunned, so guests may need to remember this ingrained cultural habit. There are also traditional ideas about eating certain foods at particular times – e.g. it is considered unwise to take milk or citrus fruit when suffering from a cough.

DRESS

Most South Asians dress with modesty. This can be interpreted in a number of ways. People may cover their heads, especially in places of worship. This is especially true of women, particularly married women. Women will usually cover their legs as well. South Asians, especially those from the older generation, are often reluctant to undress in front of, or be handled by, medical staff, especially those of the opposite sex. They would generally prefer to be treated by those of the same gender. Jewellery and other articles about the person, such as bangles, threads and turbans, should be treated with respect, as these items often carry religious or cultural significance.

FAMILY

South Asians tend to share certain family values. Emphasis is placed on the importance of the family. The elder generation is respected, and usually looked after in the home. Families often live in extended relationships, with several generations, and sisters' and brothers' families, living together in one house. Although family planning is becoming more acceptable, abortion is generally frowned upon. Fertility is privileged, and for many it is particularly important to have a son to carry on the family name. Relatives of the mother are often anxious to see that she has 40 days rest after giving birth, and may worry if she has to get up for a bath within the first few days, for example. Divorce, though not forbidden by any of the religions, often carries social stigma, and is avoided. Pre- and extra- marital sex are generally not condoned, and married couples are less likely than westerners to indulge in public displays of affection. Arranged marriages are common, but all of the religions state that they should not take place without the consent of both parties.

GENDER

Although customs are changing, people are often still expected to follow specific gender roles. Women increasingly work, but are frequently also expected to fulfil a domestic function. This is a valued role, however, and does not mean that they are considered inferior. Women are the primary educators of children, and so are often the most devout followers of their religions. Both Sikhism and Islam state that women and men are equal, and Islamic law protects the rights of married women to retain their own name and property, to be able to be educated and to work, and still be financially supported by their husbands. Some separation of the sexes takes place, particularly in places of worship. In some Muslim homes women have their own quarters and will not see men who are not family members. This separation means that certain western tactile forms of communication may not be considered acceptable, or may cause discomfort, to some people of South Asian origin.

HEALTH

Since Indian food is rich in saturated fats, people from the subcontinent tend to suffer more with food-related disorders, such as heart disease, diabetes, obesity and strokes. Although all the religions discourage the consumption of alcohol and tobacco, this is not borne out socially in the UK. For example, in certain British Muslim communities, nearly half the male population smokes. Some of these same communities are 2 to 3 times more physically inactive and obese than the national average. South Asians generally prefer to wash in free-flowing water (showers not baths), so will need this provided for them if they are in hospital.

IN THE HOME

Since many South Asians sit on the floor, they will usually wish visitors to remove their shoes before entering their house. Hindus may have a shrine for worship in their homes, and any religious items should be treated with respect. Social customs regarding the importance of hospitality are upheld vigorously, and it may be considered offensive for visitors to refuse refreshments when offered.

SPIRITUALISTS

Modern Spiritualism began in March 1848 in New York State as a result of the psychic experiences of the Fox family. The first Spiritualist Church in UK was opened in Keighley, Yorkshire in 1853. The Spiritualists' National Union Ltd. Was formed in 1901. It acts as a trustee and support to the churches and provides educational courses.

Spiritualism is based on seven basic principles: the Fatherhood of God, the Brotherhood of Man, the Communion of Spirits and the Ministry of Angels, the Continuous Existence of the Human Soul, Personal Responsibility, Compensation and Retribution Hereafter for all the Good or Evil Deeds done on Earth, Eternal Progress Open to every Human Soul.

Spiritualism is a universal religion which recognises such leaders as the Buddha, Mohammed, Moses and Jesus and considers them great healers and teachers. The main difference between Spiritualism and some other religions is that it is founded on the demonstrated proof that there is life after death and that there is a path of eternal progression for all mankind with an acceptance of responsibility for one's own actions.

ETHICAL TEACHING

We are all part of a divine plan involving the whole universe. Spiritualism is concerned with the way we live here and now. We should live harmoniously with others doing unto others as we would have others do to us.

MEDIUMS

The work of a medium is to prove the reality of survival after so-called death and to pass on practical help and understanding when needed. The advice given should add meaning and a deeper sense of purpose to life.

SPIRITUAL HEALING

Spiritual healing is practised in churches and centres. It can assist treatment given by doctors and may cure illnesses which fail to respond to other forms of treatment. It is administered by the laying on of hands – contact healing – and should not be confused with faith healing.

WORSHIP

Church Services are conducted with reverence. An address is given on the philosophy of Spiritualism and it is normally followed by a demonstration to prove the reality of survival.

TAOISTS

Taoism/Daoism is generally thought to have begun with the writings of Lao-Tsu, a man from China who is attributed with writing the Tao te Ching, or the Book of the Way and its Power, some time between 604-531 BCE. It was adopted as the state religion of China in 440 CE, but ceased to be so in 1911.

Tao' means 'the Way', and the first cause of the universe: the force that flows through all life. It is the producer and source of order and stability. Taoists seek to live in harmony with that force, by leading a balanced life. Taoism is thus a nature-based philosophy, embodying four principles: Oneness (which starts and ends with the observation of nature), Dynamic Balance, Complementary Cycles and Harmonious Action. For Taoists time is cyclical, not linear as in western thinking.

The principles of Dynamic Balance and Complementary Cycles are embodied in the symbol of the Yin-Yang, which depicts the two opposite energies from whose interaction the universe is believed to have emerged. When these opposites are equally present, everything is calm, which is where the Taoist emphasis on balance comes from. This is also seen in the elements of fire, water, wood, metal and earth, which should be balanced wherever possible to create fortune, as well as in the practice of feng shui, which aims to balance the way the home is set out, in order to generate greater prosperity.

Taoism encourages its followers to accept life, with its good and its bad. It teaches that most suffering and weakness comes from resistance to natural processes. This is evident in the principle of Harmonious Action, which can be illustrated by the example of a bamboo stick bending with the wind. It overcomes the wind by yielding to it. If it were stiff it would break, but because it yields it overcomes. This can also be expressed in the art of wu wei, which is to let nature take its course, but also to be kind to other people because such actions are reciprocated.

Another Taoist principle is that each person has a life force (known as Chi) that should be looked after, and so health is considered very important. An individual's chief task is to develop their virtue – especially the three jewels of compassion, moderation and humility.

Taoism emphasises the individual's responsibility to react to the situation, and is more concerned with guidelines for harmonious living than rules. Matters of dress etc are, therefore, determined by the culture of the person concerned.

Taoists do not pray, rather they seek to answer life's problems through inner meditation and outer observation. Many Taoists practice Tai Chi, which is a slow, controlled technique of movement and breathing.

Many Taoists believe in spirits of nature, or personified deities. Some may not believe in these as actual entities, but as symbols that help them to understand the world around them.

Most Taoists are of Chinese origin. However, increasing numbers of Westerners are becoming influenced by Taoist principles.

TRAVELLER GYPSIES

The Traveller Gypsies, or Romanichals, are a semi-nomadic people with a distinct lifestyle. Scholars differ as to the origins of the Gypsy people, with some tracing them to India, but Gypsies in every country have intermingled with the majority culture, and so the race is not as distinct as is sometimes thought. Often a Gypsy is identified as such on cultural, rather than purely ethnic, grounds. Since their arrival in England in the 16th century, Traveller Gypsies' strong sense of identity and separateness has been maintained by the experience of persecution. They are often suspicious of bureaucracy and institutions.

Irish Travellers came to England in the mid 19th century to take advantage of economic opportunities. Their origins can be found in early Irish history. Invasion and famine caused many sedentary families to lead a nomadic lifestyle. Intermarriage with the indigenous Travellers has led to a community with a distinct culture.

'Gypsy Traveller' is a term that covers a range of disparate groups, with different cultural traditions. For example, there are New Travellers, who have adopted a nomadic lifestyle out of choice, and who may not follow much Gypsy tradition. There are also Occupational Travellers, such as circus and fairground workers. According to the Traveller Law Research Unit in Cardiff, there are about 300,000 Gypsies and Travellers in Britain today. They are a difficult group to quantify however, especially as some may hide their identity, fearing discrimination.

In recent years many have adapted to meet the demands made by economic and social change, from living in wagons drawn by horses to travelling in modern trailer caravans; from earning a living doing farm work, fruit picking and hawking handmade goods to collecting scrap metal, tarmacking, tree pruning etc. Legislation has made it more difficult to live a mobile lifestyle and many families have been forced to settle on permanent sites or to move into houses. There is also variation in lifestyle through choice, with some Travellers being generally mobile, others travelling seasonally, and others being mostly sedentary. Distances travelled vary from weekend visits, to traditional horse fairs, to intercontinental journeys.

Many adult Travellers have not had the opportunity to attend school and are non-literate. Some cannot tell the time. Documentation (such as birth certificates) may not be readily available. Children are taught the skills to support their lifestyle within the family by example and practice.

Gypsies have their own language, which is called Romanes. They also have their own words for certain things: e.g. non-Gypsies are called Gorgios. It is important to remember that some Travellers consider their language and many of their traditions as secret, and no business of Gorgios.

DEATH

In hospital, the dying will be visited as often as possible, regardless of hospital rule. Death should be witnessed by spouse and by other next of kin. When a Gypsy dies it is common practice for a wake to be held. The coffin is placed in the trailer caravan with the lid open for friends and family to pay their last respects. The release of the spirit or the 'mulla' is seen as important and the deceased person's caravan will be burnt and possessions smashed so there are no personal items the spirit might cling to thus preventing the spirit's release. Some Gypsies will not say the name of a dead person. All friends and relatives attend the funeral; sometimes several hundred mourners will be present. Elaborate wreaths are commissioned in the shape of the deceased person's favourite possessions: a dog, a lorry, or even a bottle of Guinness! Graves are visited regularly by surviving relatives and fresh flowers laid. Traditionally the location of death would be avoided by close relatives for a year or more.

DIET

Many Travellers will not eat hospital food, nor food offered to them in Gorgio households, for fear of it being 'unclean'. They prefer to eat food prepared for them by people they know.

DRESS

Traditional Gypsy women dress modestly, with legs covered. Often they will also have heads and arms covered. Gold jewellery worn is a symbol of status and wealth.

FAMILY LIFE

The Traveller community is comprised of extended family groups and affiliates in which family ties are strong. Each family speaks for itself – there are few community leaders, although old age is respected. Marriages between affiliated groups, often at a young age, can be popular. Children are highly valued, cared for and protected. Living in trailer caravans means that extended family members can stop together, the men often forming work partnerships and the women supporting each other in the care of children and other activities. Men and women have a distinct and closely defined gender role within the community.

Visitors should wait to be invited into a trailer by the occupant, who may prefer to talk outside the family home. They should avoid any mention of anything at all sexual or related to bodily functions. If tea is offered it should be accepted as it is a sign of acknowledgement of the family's cleanliness and also of acceptance by the family of the visitor.

HYGIENE

Traditionally there have been strict rules about hygiene. The customs are known as 'mochadi' (ritually unclean) as opposed to 'chikli' (merely dusty or acceptably dirty). Most of these rules derive from a strict separation of inner and outer – e.g. the area outside of a trailer can be untidy or dirty so long as the inside is clean. Food preparation techniques are of utmost importance. For instance it is 'mochadi' to have a toilet in a caravan where food is prepared or to wash one's body or hands in a bowl for washing crockery. Tea towels are washed in a separate bowl and a menstruating woman might not be permitted to prepare food. In some families cats are seen as 'mochadi', and dogs would not be allowed in the home. It is ironic that whilst Gypsies have often been stereotyped as unclean by the majority culture, Gypsies are just as likely to consider Gorgio practices unclean.

MARRIAGE

In past years marriages might have been arranged – often between 1st or 2nd cousins – to strengthen family ties. Sometimes a couple would 'run away' together. Today young people usually choose their own partner. Marriages are an opportunity to bring friends and family together and take place in a church or registry office.

MEDICINE

In the past Traveller Gypsies were skilled in the preparation of herbal cures for most diseases and illnesses. These may still be used by the older generation, but most Travellers use conventional medical treatments today, although it can be difficult seeing a doctor or keeping appointments at a hospital if you have no legal place to stop. If a Traveller is hospitalised expect many people to turn up to visit – especially if a new baby has been born! Some Gypsies think of hospitals as concentrations of Gorgio disease and will only resort to using a hospital in emergencies – for instance when a baby needs treatment. However, since hospitals are seen as polluted, places of death and disease, they are the best place for handling the rites of passage that Gypsies see as most polluting – childbirth and death.

Many Travellers, particularly men, are heavy smokers. As intermarriage is common, there is a higher risk of chromosomal recessive disorders. Sometimes standard immunisations are not carried out, so there may be a higher rate of tetanus, polio and tuberculosis.

NAMES

An individual may use either of their parents' surnames dependent upon the situation. Strangers should be guided by the individual as to how they would like to be known.

PREJUDICE

With the membership of the four new Eastern European states into the EU, Gypsy Travellers have become the largest ethnic minority in the EU. Despite this, Gypsies and Travellers may experience much social exclusion. Members of the Traveller community may experience problems such as high infant mortality rates, low life expectancy, poor accommodation provision by public service providers and negative press coverage.

PRIVACY

Travellers place a high value on privacy, and confidentiality should be preserved.

RELIGION

Travellers usually adopt the religion of the country in which they live. Therefore most Gypsies in the UK are Christian. In recent years evangelical Christianity, particularly the 'Gypsies for Christ' movement, has won many converts. Irish Travellers follow the Catholic traditions.

VIETNAMESE

Most Vietnamese people in Britain are refugees who have fled from persecution in North Vietnam and are Chinese in origin. Their background is roughly 80% Buddhist and 20% Catholic. Ancestor-worship is also practised. The traditional languages are Vietnamese and Cantonese. The elderly may hold on to traditional practices and not speak English. As a result of 30 years of Communist domination, the younger generation has missed out on the traditional formation of religious practices and devotion.

BIRTH

Mother and baby stay at home for the first month after birth. At the end of this period a special meal is held in celebration.

DEATH

Traditionally, when a member of the family dies, the body is laid out at home for 1-3 days before the funeral. During this period offerings of food and drink are made to the soul of the deceased. For Catholics, masses would normally be said by a Catholic priest in church. White is the colour of mourning.

DIET

Vietnamese eat a lot of fresh fruits and salads. Some do not take dairy products. Some will not eat lamb. Vietnamese Buddhists are often vegetarian. Vietnamese tend to prefer noodles and rice to potatoes. Those who are Catholics may refuse to eat meat on Fridays. Most have got used to English cups of tea!

DRESS

Western dress is usually worn but the Ao Dai may be worn on special occasions. This traditional dress is a high-necked, close-fitting garment, with a side slit.

FAMILY LIFE

Three generations traditionally live together, sharing responsibility for the care of the young, the old and the sick. The absence of close family networks helps to explain the extreme sense of loss felt by many Vietnamese people in Britain, particularly those who came to the UK alone.

FASTING

The Catholic Vietnamese normally observe Lenten and Good Friday fasts.

FESTIVALS

Tet is the Vietnamese New Year, at which time presents and money are exchanged. The Moon Festival (usually late Aug/ early Sep) celebrates the new moon, but this is not widely observed in Britain.

GREETING

The older generation of Vietnamese usually greet with a slight bow, rather than with a handshake. Vietnamese culture in general is not tactile: hugging and kissing are reserved for the privacy of families.

IN A VIETNAMESE HOME

It is usual to remove the shoes on entering the home. It may be impolite to refuse refreshments.

MEDICINE

There are no specific objections to blood transfusions and transplants. However there is generally great apprehension about operations and the giving of blood samples. In Vietnam, much higher dosages of antibiotics may be prescribed. Therefore Vietnamese people may feel the lower dosage prescribed in the UK does not have the same effect.

MODESTY

Vietnamese women are generally rather shy and would prefer to be examined by a female doctor.

NAMES AND TITLES

Traditionally the family name comes before the personal name, but in Britain some Vietnamese reverse them. It is not always possible to determine gender from a given individual name. The titles 'brother', 'sister', 'aunt' or 'uncle' are often used as a substitute for 'Mr' or 'Mrs'. The relative ages of the people concerned determines whether someone is addressed as 'aunt' or 'sister', 'uncle' or 'brother'. Vietnamese women do not usually take their husband's name. There are only about 25 Vietnamese family names.

SICK VISITING

Vietnamese Catholics would need the ministry of a Catholic priest and would be shocked if a lay woman brought Communion to them.

ZOROASTRIANS

Zoroastrianism is based on the teachings of Zarathushtra. Although chronology and location are uncertain, it is now generally accepted that he lived c1200 BCE, and that he spread his message in Persia (now Iran). The followers of his tradition, who are mostly now in India after fleeing Islamic persecution in the ninth century CE, are often known as "Parsis", which means "Persians". The main doctrine espoused by Zarathushtra, or Zoroaster as he is sometimes called, was monotheism. This had a major influence on other religions, particularly the Abrahamic faiths.

Despite this monotheism, many of the ancient gods of the Iranian pantheon filtered back into Zoroastrianism after his death as holy spirits, or yazatas. There is also a later strain of the religion that is almost dualist in form, in that it makes the spirit of evil independent of God, and co-eternal with him. Zoroastrianism stresses the free will of all humans to choose good or bad. In this later belief-system, even God, Ahura Mazdah, pronounces his deliberate choice of good over evil. Goodness is therefore never to be taken for granted, but is always something that must be striven for over evil. Zoroastrianism is based on a series of firm binary oppositions - good/evil, truth/untruth, order/disorder.

ABLUTIONS
Hands and faces are washed before worship, and shoes are removed before entering the temple.

CHARITY
Hospitality to strangers, and active concern for the underprivileged are central tenets of Zoroastrianism.

DEATH
Zoroastrians see the world as a transitory abode, and believe that individuals will receive reward or punishment in the afterlife. This is envisioned in two symbols. The first is the Cinvat bridge, or Bridge of the Requiter, which the bad cannot pass, but fall into the mud of the abyss. The second is the image of molten metal, in which souls are tested. It destroys the bad, but to the good it is like a bath in warm milk.

One exceptional belief of Zoroastrianism is that resurrection (Frashkart) at the end of the world will be in spirit and body, and that it will be for all – sinners will be freed from hell. Zoroastrianism holds that the soul of the departed hovers near the body for three days. Death is seen as the triumph of evil, and so a corpse is considered to be polluting. It should therefore be disposed of as quickly as possible.

The traditional method of disposal in India would be to expose the corpse in a "Tower of Silence" (daxma) for vultures to eat. This is because Zoroastrians do not want to pollute fire or earth or water with their bodies. This can create problems for British Zoroastrians, who, if not flying the body back to India, must adapt their practice to suit available options. Cremation, as the socially acceptable norm in India, is likely to be preferred to burial. Ashes will usually be interred at the Zoroastrian cemetery at Brookwood in Surrey.

Zoroastrian funerals are simple – Zoroastrians believe charity in memory of the deceased is more effective than elaborate, costly funeral rites. Ancestor-worship also plays an important part in Zoroastrianism.

DRESS

The wearing of traditional symbols of faith has declined, but Zoroastrians may wear the sudreh and kusti. The sudreh is a sacred shirt, like a white vest, symbolising purity and renewal. The kusti is a long cord tied round the waist. It has seventy-two strands, symbolising the seventy-two chapters of the holy book, the Yasna, as well as universal fellowship. The sudreh and kusti are both seen as protection against evil, and are thought of as being the armour and sword-belt of Zoroastrians, arming them for the battle against evil.

EMPLOYMENT

Zoroastrians in Britain are often involved in law and medicine, or the textile trade. 72% of British Zoroastrians have a university degree; so they comprise a very highly educated population.

ETHICS

As in many other religions, "Do in holiness anything you will" is the golden rule. A strict adherence to truth is central to the faith, since lies are thought to belong to the realm of evil. Scrupulous honesty in business dealings is practised.

FAMILY PLANNING

Zoroastrianism is not an ascetic religion – it believes all material things to have been created by Ahura Mazdah for enjoyment. Zoroastrians have reverence for physical things, especially those that are in their purest or most natural forms, such as the elements. It is considered a primal duty to assist life's fertility wherever possible, both within the family unit, and in a wider social context. For early Zoroastrians, this meant being good husbandmen to the land, as well as being parents – farming was revered. However, Zoroastrianism also stresses purity and control, so promiscuity and prostitution are unacceptable. British Zoroastrians almost always have small families – rarely more than two children. Perhaps because of the small numbers of Zoroastrians, and because of their history of religious persecution, resistance to intermarriage is high.

FESTIVALS

There are seven main festivals, each relating to major spirits that are worshipped – the six Amesha Spentas, or Holy Immortals, and Ahura Mazdah himself. These seven spirits together are known as the divine Heptad, and each is responsible for a certain area of creation. The seven festivals culminate with No Ruz, or New Day, which prefigures the New Day at the end of the world when creation will be transformed, and the dead be resurrected. Since different traditions adopted different calendars, the dates of these festivals vary. There are also minor festivals, but it is the observance of these seven that is obligatory.

FOOD

Zoroastrian festivals celebrate the material, so feasting plays an important part. The feasts cross class boundaries, with rich and poor eating together. It is considered a sin to fast, since to do so weakens the body, and also one's resistance to evil. Often ceremonial foods will revolve around the number seven (such as having seven kinds of dried fruits and nuts), with reference to the divine Heptad. Zarathushtra declaimed against drunkenness, and advocated moderation. There are no specific dietary restrictions, but some Zoroastrians interpret their religion as advocating the avoidance of pork and beef, or as advising vegetarianism.

NATURE

Zoroastrians have particular reverence for cattle. Additionally, they believe that humankind, as the pinnacle of creation, and the only creatures capable of deliberate choice, should care for the world to the best of their capabilities.

RITUAL

Fire plays an important role in Zoroastrian ritual. It is seen as the symbol of Ahura Mazdah, and also as the formless living symbol of the source of heat and life. Zoroastrians are often called "fire worshippers", but find this deeply offensive.

RITES OF PASSAGE

Before puberty, between the ages of seven and twelve, young Zoroastrians take part in a Navjote ceremony, in which they symbolically take on the responsibility of upholding Zoroastrianism.

POSTSCRIPT

This handbook only attempts to offer basic information on religious and cultural issues. More details can be found in the extensive literature on the subject and on the internet (though this needs to be used with discernment).

Most localities throughout the UK have inter-faith groups who organise open meetings and events and whose members are willing to share information and to give talks about their faiths. The Inter-Faith Network UK is a good source of information about these local groups.

There is a growing interest among the general public in studying religious diversity for its own sake. Many organisations offer taught courses on the subject and some institutions provide distance learning courses.

Many institutions including colleges, hospitals and prisons are developing multi-faith chaplaincies. These initiatives can be grounded in the local community and become centres of creativity and growth.

The new human rights legislation requires organisations to be better informed on faith issues. SIFRE has experience in Diversity Training and is able to arrange courses to suit particular needs. SIFRE's board game Diversity enables people to explore issues around faith and culture in an enjoyable and non-threatening way. This, together with many other resources, is available from The Festival Shop whose extensive catalogue is available on request.